AF520341

Inside the Indian Army

Attention Authors

Manas Publications is fighting a war to tell the world that India can win the battle not only by the bullet but also by pen. We are converting fighters into writers. There is no dearth of intellectuals in our country, however, their knowledge is confined to them only. No sincere effort has been made by any other publisher to channelise their knowledge, that is why the talent of every intellectual remains latent. An author always presents the raw material in the shape of a manuscript and it is the job of the publisher to convert it into a finished product. Manas has been continually motivating intellectuals and publishing their manuscripts for more than two decades and would like to publish your manuscript too. If you or your colleagues have a manuscript ready for publication or are working on it, contact us with a detailed synopsis and list of contents. Manas can also suggest you a suitable title for writing related to your area of expertise. Manas is known for its publishing quality. We take utmost care in publishing and also give wide publicity to the book and its author through our national and international distribution network.

Inside the Indian Army

Brig. Trigunesh Mukherjee, AVSM (Retd.)

Manas Publications
(We Convert Fighters into Writers)
New Delhi-110 002 (INDIA)

MANAS PUBLICATIONS
(Publishers, Library Suppliers, Importers & Exporters)
4402/5-A, Ansari Road (Opp. HDFC Bank)
Darya Ganj, New Delhi-110 002 (INDIA)
Off. ✆ 23260783, 23265523, Res. ✆ 23842660
Fax: 011-23272766
E-mail: manaspublications@vsnl.com
manaspublications@yahoo.com

© Brig. Trigunesh Mukherjee, AVSM (Retd.)

Second Impression 2011 (2000)

ISBN 81-7049-073-1
Rs 495

No part of this book can be reproduced, stored in a retrieval system, or transmitted in any form, by any means, including mechanical, electronic, photocopying, recording, or otherwise, without prior written permission of the publisher.

The views expressed in this book are those of the author and not at all of the publisher. The publisher is not responsible for the views of the author and authenticity of the data, in any way whatsoever.

Typeset at
Manas Publications

Printed in India at
R.K. Offset Works, Delhi
and Published by Mrs. Suman Lata for
Manas Publications, 4402/5-A, Opp HDFC Bank,
Ansari Road, Daryaganj
New Delhi 110002 (INDIA)

Preface

Towards the end of 1946 and in 1947 Lieutenant General (then Brig) Nathu Singh [who was earmarked to be the first Commander in Chief (C in C) of free India] had written to the Defence Minister designate (Shri Baldev Singh) expressing his opposition to the partition of the country. He felt that if the Indian Army was not divided it could hold the country together. He never forgave Nehru and the others for making decisions without consulting the Army. A fact that is not well known is that Cariappa became the C in C as officers junior to him (who were preferred by the politicians) declined the selection to become C in C over Cariappa in keeping with the tradition of seniority.

> "Positive contribution of the Indian Military is the consistent professional support they have given to Indian democracy"
> \- *Stephen Cohen*

> "......In fact, apart from the army there is no neutrality left in the civil society."
>
> *- Lord Meghnad Desai talking about India in an interview published in Business India*

This book is written because there are still a large number of Indians whose chests swell when the National Anthem is played, because the unsung heroes of this country deserve to be written about, because people have a right to know about their Army, because we need to learn that not all our enemies are beyond our borders, and because the powers that be do not care. The Army works on indefatigably but rewards and recognition from the political bosses, in particular and the country in general are, at best, absent. One must hastily add that the common man, especially those whose lives have been touched by the Army, has nothing but praise for the armyman.

The Army is apparently the last resort for everything if these newspaper headlines are anything to go by :

"Army helps movement of essential goods"

"Let the Army take charge of traffic"

"Army begins rescue work"

"Army called out in Bihar, MP"

"Centre to seek Army help to deal with postal strike"

"Army steps in, telecom talks fall through"

"Bombed passengers praise armymen"

In a survey conducted by Gallup in 1996, sixty-three percent interviewees expressed faith in the Armed Forces while about forty-eight percent vouched for the Supreme Court and police departments drew "no confidence".

A special report published in January 1999 (The Times of India) also brought to light some interesting findings about the Armed Forces :-

(Ranking of 1 to 16 was worked out for different professions; the Armed Forces rankings are shown below)

Which in your opinion is the most respected profession? 1

Given the choice which profession would you choose? 2

Contributes the most to society?

5

Deserves better recognition and incentives? 1

The Army is a large and complex organisation and one book cannot cover it all. A fond hope is that this book will encourage people to ask questions. We are talking about the largest volunteer Army in the world and it is dependent on a democracy to give it a fair deal; and people make a democracy. Criticism should be welcome as long as the Army gets a fair deal at the end of it all. Corporate bodies, railways, policy makers et al need to increase their objectivity in dealing with the armyman ..... and not make travel a nightmare; not dole out underpaid jobs; not let them down with poor decisions etc.

It is also time for the Army to get its act together and take a few people from the media etc to court. One is sick of seeing improper representation of the Army in films, advertisements (like cap badges in the McDowell's No 1; Onida TV with JCOs wearing cap badges worn by Colonels and above all; comic figures getting rid of blocked noses and so on), in print and by cable TV channels who simply do not bother to "learn". The Army needs to get off its laid back culture (as far as the media is concerned) and put out well produced informative pieces. Informing the public is the Army's job.

That independent India has gone past 50 with the same geographical boundaries is one of the most important contributions of the Army to this nation. And to think that all around there have been military juntas flourishing .... surely the credit has to go the maturity of the Army ..... because lack of maturity and lack of commitment have been quite prevalent. Crises, remote areas and calamities always see the Army as the first (and sometimes the only) rays of hope.

Everybody accepts the Army's contribution but nobody talks or writes about the unknown Army soldier as the personality of the last half century. This book, hopefully, will acquire for the soldier the recognition due to him.

Brig. Trigunesh Mukherjee (Retd.)

Acknowledgement

The author gratefully acknowledges all the published material that facilitated statistical reference. The author also humbly acknowledges the contribution the Indian Army has made over 32 years of commissioned service and 4 years of precommission training in shaping his life

Contents

1

Understanding National Security

(Everybody Talks But Few Comprehend)

It has become rather fashionable to talk about National Security these days, to either appear knowledgeable or to hide one's ignorance, and sometimes to hide the misdeeds of the government in power. Well, for one thing, National Security is not a holy cow. Why is it then that in India, National Security is most often linked to "lack of information" or the blanking out of information? Although one has to accept that all information cannot be loosely bandied about, surely every citizen of a democracy has a right to (and should) know what constitutes National Security. Perhaps if the subject were more familiar to people they could contribute more constructively. After all, a nation's wellbeing is every individual's concern. So long as a fairly large number of thinking Indians learn, understand and question our national concepts we will not have a bunch of pseudo-intellectuals and those who are politically attired throwing one-way missiles of wisdom at the whole nation.

One may conclude that the situation is more akin to "national deception" rather than security. Some organisations have been around for a while and one must admit the material produced by them is quite readable but that it is not universally applicable. A few NGOs have also got into the act. However, it is business for them and, therefore, papers churned out by them will always be suspect.

It is not possible to cover all the aspects of National Security in a single chapter of a book about the Army but surely some relevant points at issue would not be out of place.

Background

In 1947, politicians who were at the helm had evolved on a diet of non-violence and satyagraha, some having been political prisoners as well. Still, the numbers that could genuinely qualify (in the words of many stalwarts) to be called "freedom fighters" were not too many. This possibly explains why we did not (and still don't) understand the value of freedom from colonial rule.

India did not have a set of decision-makers that had much idea of managing violence, which is the business of war. Defence in general and the Indian Army in particular (the Navy and the Air Force were very small services then) were not understood by the people in power. In fact, at that stage it was thought the strength of the Army could be reduced to a mere lakh. The primary task was to integrate the princely states. External security threats did not feature in their thinking or planning. It did not come as a surprise then that operations in Kashmir came to a sudden halt and western powers were allowed to handle matters in the Security Council with a strong bias in favour of Pakistan. The importance given to civilian domination did not allow the political decision-makers to seek the (professional) advice of the Army. Ironical but unique – the upholders of non-violence had to take decisions concerning the management of violence. The lingering problem is there for all to see. As is the immense number of human lives lost as a direct result of inadequate decision-making.

The government was ill-equipped to handle security problems both organisationally as well as from the angle of the decision-making process. Unfortunately, no major changes for the positive have taken place in this area over the past 50 years. If anything, matters have become worse. Unlike major democracies the world over, the armed forces in India were (still are) not integrated with the government. There seem to have been some totally unfounded fears about the armed forces upsetting the power balance. Intelligence (of various kinds) is critical for all kinds of planning but we still do not have a systematic process of intelligence assessment. In reality, what happened was that new organisations came up without any cost effectiveness studies basically to cater to short-term gains of sections of people. And as is common in bureaucrat democracies, accountability and responsibility have become progressively diluted. Failure of intelligence has plagued us since the time of Independence. If Indian intelligence organisations had done their jobs the fiasco in Sri Lanka (OP PAWAN), and, in recent times Kargil, could have been averted.

It, of course, did not help when prominent leaders gave statements like "the Army should now get down to agricultural and developmental activities to remove apprehensions from people's minds", "the Army in peace time is better utilised for farming" and so on. A sort of an expectation that the Indian Army should make amends for all that they did under British rule. Needless to say, not a single leader was clear as to what exactly was expected of the Army. This, in a democracy, is unpardonable.

The seeds of ad hoc working were well sown in the early days. Manipulation was also not unknown (a case in point could be the efforts made to keep Field Marshal Cariappa from becoming the first Commander in Chief). However, one must hastily add that there was a fairly free flow of communication between the Defence Minister of the Interim government and even some senior officers regarding the ills of partition. Contrast this with the unsavory Admiral Vishnu Bhagwat episode in recent times.

Since all matters relating to defence were handled by the British till the time of Independence they effectively sabotaged the growth of defence thinking in India. From this brief review, it can easily be seen that lack of concern of the political leaders only made things worse.

As has been well recorded in a great deal of books, the impact of the casual treatment meted out to the defence was properly felt in 1962. The political hierarchy and the bureaucracy were wholly responsible but the price, in lives, had to be paid by the Indian Army. Given the combat ratio and lack of preparedness (thanks again to the absence of vision on the part of the government) the Army performed well: any serious military historian will bear witness to this. To make matters worse (also indicating a complete lack of understanding of defence by Nehru and company) personal likes thrust senior officers onto the Indian Army whose experience was with the Army Service Corps and not with any combat arms.

Borrowing from Liddelhart – "Why don't we learn from history"? A million people could say that again but the Indian government, particularly the bureaucracy, since politicians only hold temporary assignments, remains unwilling to learn.

Concepts and Basis

National Security quite simply deals with the concepts of "nation" and "security" in the same breath. A nation's wellbeing and a continuation in that very state provide it with national security. While the defence forces provide an important prop to national security they form only a part. The involvement is far more complex and interwoven. Common culture and heritage normally support the concept of a nation. State is a political entity in terms of boundary and government. A nation state, therefore, amalgamates the spread of culture and is politically convenient. Nationalism stems from the concept of a nation state (territory, homeland, tradition, arts, literature etc) and sometimes from fear of an enemy. Heterogeneous nations will, at times, have ethnic groups thinking of nationhood which will be contained by the categorisation of "enemy" in specific terms. India has never spelt out "enemy". Nationalism, sovereignty and acceptance by international law provide a strong base for national security. There are some important ingredients that are intimately linked to national security:-

* Geography
* Economy
* Population
* Technology
* Ideology
* Morale and Will
* Leadership

Military Strength

The cascade that one should keep in mind would flow something like this:

National Interests

↓

National Objectives

↓

Environment Scan & Threat Analysis

↓

National Aims

↓

National Strategy

↙ ↓ ↘

Political | Military | Economic

↓

Military Objectives

↓

Strategic Concepts

↓

Military Capability

Force Structure

A nation's wellbeing is as good as it is perceived to be and is directly related to **"Perceived Power"**. The equation given below is interesting in many ways:

Pp = (C+E+M+S) x W

Pp : Perceived Power
C : Critical Mass (Population and Territory)
E : Economic Capability
M : Military Capability
S : Strategic Purpose
W : Will to Pursue National Strategy

A brief mention of the elements of power would be useful in our quest to understand national security:

Tangible	**Intangible**
*Population	*Leadership
*Geography	*Social Cohesiveness
*Economic Development	*History & reputation
*Military Power	*Foreign Support & Dependence
*Natural Resources	*Type of Government
*Education	*Morale
*Science & Technology	*Ideology

From perusing the above (which is not even the tip of the iceberg) it will be clear that governments have come and gone without coming to terms with the intricacies of national security thinking leave alone planning. The other point that needs to be driven home is the integrated network needed to support national security plans cutting across departments, regions, levels and so on.

If national interests, objectives and aims have never been stated by India how does one expect to view national security objectively and comprehensively? Perhaps some pundits in the North and South Blocks and many Bhawans have these secrets well hidden - so well hidden that they cannot find them and gross ignorance is hidden behind "....... may compromise national security".

Fifty years and more of independence have taught us very little. We still do not have a set of National Security Objectives clearly laid down let alone National Interests, National Objectives etc. The Armed Forces have derived objectives for their own working. But, in a democracy, the "civilian government" (as if the armed forces personnel are not part of the country and government) is required to lay these down unambiguously and give them some permanence, periodically reviewing them "objectively". These cannot change on the basis of the donning of different hues of the government in power or on the mere whims and fancies of leaders.

2

Structure and Channels

(Organisation)

The Indian Army is not really a single institution even though there are certain values, elements of culture and tradition that are universally applicable. It is more a conglomerate of institutions, all working together to create a whole which is kept together by unique bonds and variety. It would be impossible to put down in one book (or set of books) the variety that exists in the Indian Army; therefore only the general aspects are covered here.

The process of creating organisation is completely need based in the Army. This is quite unlike what happens elsewhere: an appointment is created or a committee nominated after which the organisation gets added on; and to keep it going the work keeps on getting stretched. For instance, the most basic organisation in the Army is the Infantry section. To overcome an enemy position a combat ratio of 3:1, at the least, has to be created. Therefore, at least six people are required to charge the enemy trench. If six people are assaulting, at least two are required to provide fire support. And, since fire support is a crucial area, there has to be someone in charge - in this case a junior NCO. Yet another NCO, someone reasonably senior, is required to exercise overall command and lead the assault. In this manner, a section consists of 10 people including the section commander.

Assault Group	**Support Group**
6 soldiers to Assault	2 soldiers man the Automatic Weapon
1 NCO as Commander	1 junior NCO.

Similar logic applies to all organisations in the Army. However, one has to be candid and accept that sometimes structures are tampered with simply because this is the easier way out. Since it is not possible to make any government see sense and revert to protocol seniority of the '50's or earlier, the Army tries (mostly in vain) to create more senior appointments. A case in point would be the command of units shifting to Colonels instead of Lieutenant Colonels

The basic structure was initially triangular in nature but certain variations were accepted to allow for better command and control and to get some senior ranks for the Army. One notable exception is the "four" rifle companies in Infantry battalions (though there have been many efforts to tamper with these for some absurd shortsighted gains). Needless to say, people who did not have to fight Infantry battles suggested these.

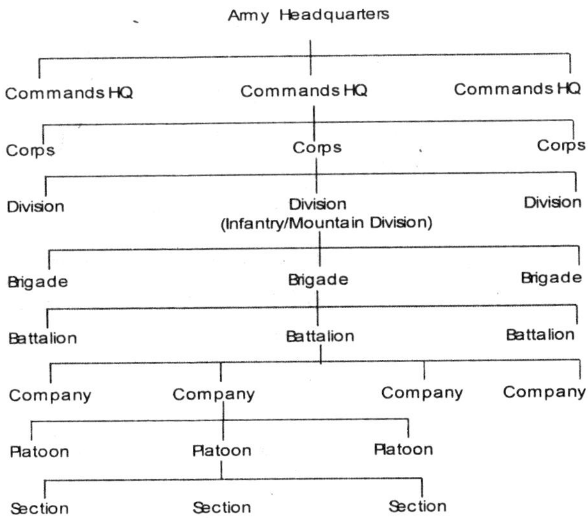

Operational needs, spread of deployment, training needs and various other factors have resulted in the following commands:-

* **Eastern Command**
* **Western Command**
* **Northern Command**
* **Southern Command**
* **Central Command**
* **Training Command**

(The last is not an operational command. Each command is headed by a Lieutenant General (Lt. Gen.) who is the General Officer Commanding in Chief (or GOC in C), also called the Army Commander).

Corps are also commanded by Lieutenant Generals and they are referred to as General Officer Commanding (GOC).........40 Corps etc or Corps Commander. Divisions are commanded by Major Generals (Maj. Gen.) and they are referred to as GOC 56 Infantry Division etc or Divisional Commander (normally abbreviated to Div Commander).

Brigadiers command brigades (in some armies around the world they are known as Brigadier Generals or one-star generals) and they are normally known as Commander 821 Mountain Brigade and so on. Battalions are also referred to as units and are commanded by Colonels. They are known as Commanding Officers or COs followed by the name of their unit (such as CO 4 RAJ RIF or 4 Rajputana Rifles). Following these, we have the Company, Platoon and Section Commanders.

To fight effectively, a balanced force is needed. The right mix of the main fighting arm with supporting arms and services achieves this. At this stage we will only state that the lowest level at which all support is available is the Division and, therefore, it is considered a tactical formation.

What then are the arms and services?

Combat Arms

The Infantry: Known as the Queen of the Battle and takes the heaviest load of fighting because of "contact" battle. In the Indian context, in a "no war" situation virtually all combat duties (fighting insurgency, terrorism, controlling the line of control, occupying the piquets along the border including Siachen and so on) fall to their lot. The Infantry also takes up the bulk of "relief" duties (Flag March, Natural Calamities, etc). They normally fight on their feet though they may be transported in any fashion. The Special Forces belong to this arm but are employed differently due to their specialised training and special equipment.

The Mechanised Infantry: These are variations of the Infantry that support armoured battles and therefore have the capacity and mobility to match the armoured units. They are equipped with Infantry Combat Vehicles (ICV). Anti-Tank Guided Missile units also come (mainly) under this umbrella.

The Armoured Corps: The glamour boys of the Army in their tanks and other support equipment. They specialise in tank battles. Units are called regiments. [The only horsed cavalry in the world, currently in service, is 61 CAVALRY. Because of their origins, 61 CAV is part of the Armoured Corps*]

Supporting Arms

The Artillery: Provides both the Infantry and armoured corps with indirect fire support. For this the Artillery is appropriately equipped with field guns, mountain guns, medium guns, heavy mortars, howitzers, heavy guns, rockets, missiles etc. To support the armoured columns with matching mobility the Artillery has Self-Propelled (SP) guns. Commonly referred to as the "gunners" units are regiments.

The Engineers: (Also referred to as the "sappers") Combat engineer tasks like bridging, track construction, mine laying (though the infantry does its own and the other arms are expected to be able to do the same), mine breaching, water supply and so on are undertaken by the sappers. Bomb disposal units are also one section that the engineers have under their wing.

---

* Corps is not to be confused with corps as a formation.

The Signals: They are responsible for all types of communication except within units. In certain armies across the world Signals is considered a service.

Air Defence Artillery: As a separate entity, AD Arty is fairly new. Earlier, it was a part of the Artillery but with greater sophistication in technology and equipment, AD Arty has become very specialised and is now an independent arm.

Army Aviation: Flying helicopters, they provide observation, reconnaissance, communication, control of artillery fire etc to the Army. Personnel basically do tenures with aviation units.

Special Units: The President's Bodyguard is a unique unit that provides security for the President. It is essentially a ceremonial unit though all personnel are also trained in airborne duties.

Services

All other branches of the Army are meant to support the fighting arms (and all other sections) logistically. The Services include:

Army Service Corps or ASC who look after food supplies and see to the fuel requirements of the Army. They also hold additional transport for movement of troops and equipment. Mules for transportation are also handled by the ASC.

Army Ordnance Corps or AOC. They procure, store and handle all kinds of equipment, from shoelaces to tanks to bridges. Ammunition is also held by the AOC (although supply forward is undertaken by ASC in times of war). In essence, the complexity and enormity of the inventory that the AOC holds is not easy to comprehend.

Army Medical Corps or AMC (Also includes the Military Nursing Service or MNS) provide all the medical assistance and healthcare that the Army needs.

Army Dental Corps or AD Corps looks after the dental needs of the Army.

Electrical and Mechanical Engineers or EME provide maintenance support to the Army for vehicles (all types), arms, instruments, optical equipment and so on. The recovery of vehicles is also an EME responsibility.

Remount and Veterinary Corps or RVC provide health care for the animals in use in the Army. Their portfolio includes breeding animals and they are also responsible for Army Dog Units.

Army Education Corps or AEC look after the educational needs of the Army. The entry level having changed to Matriculation (in most cases) the need for this corps is perhaps debatable. (More on this in a separate chapter).

Corps of Military Police or CMP are the white-belted cadre of the Army who assist in maintaining discipline, traffic control, look after Prisoners of War Camps in the line of war etc.

Judge Advocate General's Department looks after the legal needs of the Army.

Army Postal Service or APS handle all the mail for the Army. This is a very efficient organisation that draws a portion of its manpower from the postal services.

Military Farms provide the Army with their requirements of milk and other dairy products. All military farms do not keep animals - some only process the milk.

Pioneers or Corps of Pioneers: They provide manpower for operational tasks. This is to ensure that combat manpower is not diverted from its principle tasks.

Other Forces

Defence Security Corps or DSC draws its personnel from ex-servicemen. Officers are from the Army.

Rashtriya Rifles: Conceived as an additional force for counter insurgency operations. The personnel were expected to come, by and large, from among ex-servicemen. It was perhaps expected that the Ministry of Home Affairs would finance the organisation. Officers were to be deputed from the Army. Without going into details one can quote this (RR experience) as a decision made in a hurry and implemented in even greater haste. For this the Army will continue to repent at leisure. All the manpower is milked from the Army and all costs are borne by the Army.

National Security Guard or NSG does not even come under the Ministry of Defence but draws quite heavily on Army manpower.

Special Frontier Force or SFF draws a certain amount of manpower from the Army.

Assam Rifles is an organisation of the Ministry of Home Affairs but is officered mostly by the Army.

Territorial Army or TA when embodied provides an effective second tier. Some permanent staff is available from the Army and the balance arrives only when embodied.

Army Headquarters (AHQ)

The nerve centre of the Indian Army is located at New Delhi in the AHQ. Due to the lack of space, poor planning and near absence of vision, the AHQ is spread all over the place - South Block, hutments behind North Block, Sena Bhavan, piles of other hutments, R.K. Puram, Cantonment etc.

All the heads of arms and services are located at AHQ and have their respective directorates. For example, the Director General of the ASC (a Lt. Gen.) would have the Directorate (General) of ASC for all staff work regarding ASC. Depending on the size of the arm or service it will either be headed by a Lt. Gen. or Maj. Gen. (Additional Director General) or Brig. (Deputy Director General). In addition to these specific directorates there are branches and appointments which look after policy making, decision making and implementation for the Army. These are very briefly listed below:

Adjutant General's (AG's) Branch touches every individual of the Army on a day-to-day basis. This includes looking after recruitment, welfare, discipline, ceremonials, documentation, defence civilians, extra regimental employment, macro-level planning for officers and men, schools for children etc. The AG's branch also supervises all the "A" services like AMC, JAG Branch and so on.

Quarter Master General's (QMG'S) Branch looks after supplies, accommodation, land, canteen services and so on. It supervises all the "Q" services like the ASC, APS, RVC etc.

Directorate General of Military Operations (more commonly referred to as the MO Directorate) take care of the operational requirements of the Army and also conduct liaison with the Navy, Air Force and the Coast Guard.

Directorate General of Military Intelligence (or MI Directorate) is expected to coordinate the various aspects of Intelligence as applicable to the Army.

Master General of Ordnance (MGO's Branch) oversees all the equipment needs and, in effect, coordinates the working between the EME and the Ordnance.

Directorate General of Military Training (normally referred to as MT Dte. and DGMT) look after the training needs of the Army. However, with the formation of the Training Command a number of questions regarding the necessity of having two macro-level controls still remain unanswered.

Military Secretary's Branch (MS Branch) handles the posting of officers, career planning and other related issues.

Additional Directorate General of Signals Intelligence (SI Directorate) looks after the electronic intelligence requirements of the Army.

Additional Directorate General of Perspective Planning (PP Directorate) is equipped to develop strategy and visualise battle plans.

Additional Directorate General of Operational Logistics (OL Directorate) look after logistic planning to support operational plans in the Army.

Additional Directorate General of Staff Duties (ADG SD) act like a macro coordinator. They also handle movement of units and matters pertaining to restructuring etc.

Additional Directorate General of Weapons and Equipment (ADG WE) see to the evaluation, procurement and availability of weapons and equipment.

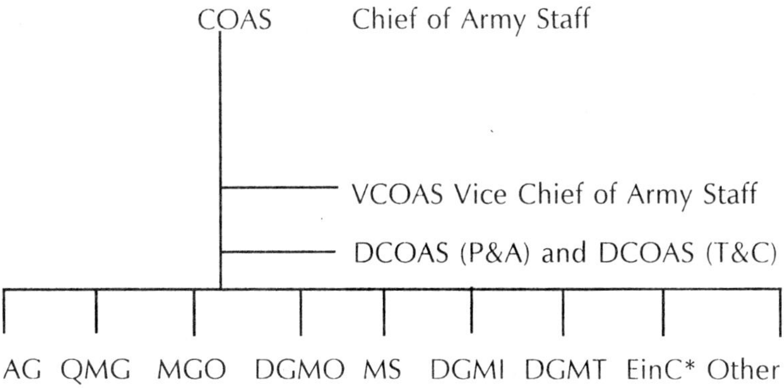

Dte.

Gen.

@ P&A -Planning & Administration

T&C- Training & Coordination.

Note: A number of directorates report (need-based) to the DCOAS/VCOAS. A strict chain of command is non-existent.

Orchestrating such a large and complex organisation in order to have it perform like a symphony is not an easy task and without fine-tuning aberrations will show. In the Army one simply cannot accept loopholes in the system because if left in the flow some vital parts could get choked. It is evident, therefore, that well educated and experienced people as well as specialists are needed to effectively oversee the functioning of the Army and other Armed Forces.

To all that has already been covered, one can include other organisations that are linked to the Army in varying degrees and the picture will need even greater focus. These

* Engineer-in-Chief

involve the Directorate General of Border Roads (DGBR), Ordnance Factories, Research and Development Organisations, Quality Assurance and so on.

Despite this scenario, the ultimate authority rests with bureaucrats and politicians who, unfortunately, are neither knowledgeable nor committed. They also have very little permanence and worse still, a complete lack of experience and exposure.

3

Free Wheeling Power

(Authority, Accountability, Responsibility)

In a democracy where the Armed Forces are not part of the governance a great deal of anomalies will inevitably occur-often to the detriment of the forces and the country at large. Most developed democracies across the world have the advantage of a fair sprinkling of genuine experience in the governing bodies (parliament, senate, defence department etc) essentially because a large number of people occupying important seats in the corridors of power have previously served in the forces. The Parliament and legislative bodies in the Indian context, however, do not have very many representatives with such experience and the few that are present do not spend either their time or energy in looking after defence interests. Lobbying is an established modus operandi in the political arena and therefore it is essential for the Army to have supportive and understanding lobbies in government and legislative bodies. Perhaps, the influence needs to be extended to other areas too like the academic world, judiciary, media and so on.

Supreme Commander

The Supreme Commander of the Armed Forces, and, therefore, of the Army, is the President of India. Commissions (parchments received by officers) are signed by the President. The appointment itself is ceremonial in nature.

Parliament

Doordarshan, with its live coverage of the goings on within Parliament, has helped in lowering the credibility of and esteem for this august body. When it comes to wielding absolute power though, Parliament reigns supreme because as a collective body it is expected to represent the nation. However, indisciplined behaviour that includes chair throwing, mike breaking, and the hurtling of abuses haven't exactly helped in the Parliament earning genuine respect for itself. Although individually some members may be mature, knowledgeable and keep the interests of the public in mind, we are repeatedly witness to thoughts, actions and policies of convenience. As far as the Army is concerned, being an apolitical body, interest in what goes on in Parliament does not arouse a great deal of interest. The fact that its votes are only postal ballots (hardly ever counted) does not help.

However, it would be a grave error to imagine that the Army (this applies to the other forces as well) is wholly indifferent to the actions and antics of our Parliament. The great variation in ethos and values (Army and Parliament as organisations) is not lost on the Army in general. The thinking people (and the numbers are not small) in the Army do keep a track of the glossy Annual Report of the MOD. Subjects of import such as the lack of debate on the defence budget, of the budget becoming smaller every year in real terms, of the parochial interests of individuals MPs/ministers which upset retirement rules, promotion policies within the Army (these and a host of others) definitely do not go unnoticed by the Army. Yet it is a fact that the Army mostly keeps mum. This is often due to a misplaced sense of loyalty and a grossly misunderstood sense of commitment to the nation. The Parliament has never bothered to discuss and analyse the reasons for the Indian Army not going the neighbours' way.

Unless allocated to one of the many committees, an MP does not have direct interaction with the Army even though occasional visits are organised (the results of these visits are not known - perhaps no one cares either)!

Cabinet

Higher defence organisation in India hopefully exists and functions in a manner it should. This skeptical opening stems from the fact that professionals are prominent through their absence. People get placed in prominent seats in the Defence Ministry simply because in the bargaining for power it inevitably suits someone or the other to put a particular person there. Fortunately, India is a country renowned for its "mystical events" and it is hoped that some of it rubs off onto those people who are suddenly catapulted to decision making on defence! Suddenly, all the wisdom of strategy, national security, vision et al get transferred to the decision-makers. Higher Defence Organisation (or control) has to effectively do the following:-

* Coordinate defence preparation and foreign policy.
* Formulate strategy at the highest level that is easily implemented.
* Create a "national will".
* During war change broad objectives where necessary.

* Sell "conduct of war" within and outside the country.

Since the Prime Minister and his council of ministers wield actual authority, de facto control rests with the defence minister or Raksha Mantri. The PM and the cabinet are at the helm and in turn pass on work to "committees" (because of this subletting, often nothing gets done!). Some of the important organisations/sub organisations are:

CCPA (Cabinet Committee on Political Affairs): Composed of the Prime Minister and a number of senior cabinet ministers. Non-member ministers attend meetings by invitation when required.

Functions of CCPA: Deal with matters related to Centre-state relationship, law and order, internal security, broad economic issues, foreign affairs including policy formulation and coordination and defence matters. (For defence per se CCPA lays down the aims and broad political and defence policy objectives).

If people wonder how much quality time CCPA can devote to defence their questioning will not be misplaced.

DMC or **RMC** (Defence Minister's Committee) is chaired by the Defence Minister or Raksha Mantri (RM). It is composed of the Minister of State for Defence (or Deputy RM), Minister of State for Defence Production, three chiefs of the Armed Forces, Defence Secretary, Scientific Advisor to the RM, Financial Advisor (Defence Services).

Functions: The committee is expected to deal with defence planning, operational intelligence, training, manpower, honours and awards, works, resettlement etc. (RMC obviously has to deal with policies and not micro issues).

Defence Minister's Production and Supply Committee: Policy matters relating to defence production and defence supplies.

Defence Research and Development Council.

Defence Minister's Appelate Committee on Pensions

War Book Committee

Chiefs of Staff Committee: Comprises the three chiefs and SA to RM (by invitation when required).

Functions. COSC is the authority for advising the RM on all defence matters and normally through him, the CCPA.

NOTE: Advisory in capabilities and with little decision-making authority (which is binding in nature) except when it affects inter-service organisations.

Defence Planning Staff: A group under COSC ostensibly to integrate the plans of the three services. However, DPS has no direct authority over the operational planners of the three services.

Defence Electronics Committee

Principal Personnel Officers' Committee

Principal Supply Officers' Committee

Joint Intelligence Committee: Composed of an Additional Secretary (chairman), a Deputy Secretary (Secretary), representatives (one each) from the ministries (Defence, External Affairs and Home Affairs), IB (Intelligence Bureau), RAW (Research and Analysis Wing), Military, Naval and Air Intelligence. It functions directly under the Cabinet Secretary.

Functions: JIC is required to present "jointly" intelligence pertaining to threats (external and internal) to CCPA, ministries, Chiefs etc.

Joint Planning Committee (JPC): Composed of Directors of Military, Naval and Air Operations.

Joint Training Committee (JTC)

Joint Sea/Air Warfare Committee (JSAWC)

There are a host of other such committees and many more which do not even feature in Higher Defence Organisation but perhaps have greater impact. For instance, the Hindi Implementation Committee, Parliamentary Committees (Standard or periodically appointed) etc.

To be effective, committees must hold meetings periodically. Contrarily, even if they do, one is left wondering as to when the concerned people work when they are only moving from meeting to meeting!

Ministry of Defence

RM (Raksha Mantri), RRM (Raksha Rajya Mantri) and RUM (Raksha Utpadan Mantri) together look after the Ministry of Defence. A few of the committees are common (the above-mentioned list) while some new ones are added on. Interestingly, the MOD does not have many files of its own - all concerned departments send comprehensive files which makes it easier to point out errors and send the cases back with queries. The major drawback is that this process delays the entire procedure (often rendering the project useless).

The stranglehold within the MOD is operated through a quadrangular concept: bureaucrats, clerical staff, processes (rules and regulations and orders) and files (queries). The normal tenure being five years, it is possible to get a few details under one's sleeve and retain them for exchange value. I'm certain the reader has got the drift! Added to this is the major issue of virtually anything and everything that is remotely important requiring the MOD's approval. The stage is set for delays, quid pro quos and wielding of undue authority.

Any query raised by the MOD sends people in Army Headquarters into a spin. More often than not queries are raised because people (it could be a section officer or an under secretary) have not even bothered to read the file. The Army's response is typical because everyone wants to get things done and people in the MOD take advantage of this. Quite obviously, very few senior officers tell people in the MOD to "please read before raising queries".

Bureaucracy

The crying need of the hour is to get specialists and professionals to oversee functions looked after by professionals. From animal husbandry to Defence or Defence to Industry or Khadi Board to Defence - the movement does not seem to matter and people suddenly become (or seem to become) knowledgeable about defence. Taking advantage of the authority reposed in them, the bureaucracy become pretenders to knowledge. Consequently, since senior officers have a lot to gain from "favourable" interaction, calling the bureaucrats' bluff is expectedly not on their agenda.

As far as holidays and travel go, it would be a lot easier to organise if solely handled by the forces. Rules and regulations can be quoted according to convenience to keep the army on the defensive. In a lighter vein, a familiar sight to behold every summer is when the job of fitting air coolers is given to contractors. At least a month of the sultry season will pass before these are functional. People who fit them are not responsible for their running; those responsible for their running are not responsible for filling of water and so on. The CAO's (Chief Administrative Officer) office can never help and so a Catch 22 situation prevails. Typically, one fine day summer will be declared officially "over" and the coolers will be removed from windows and dumped in the corridors. During the summer each office has to see that one person keeps a track of the man whose job it is to fill water in the coolers. Despite this, they will not be functional due to lack of water for two to three hours in a day. The contractor is supposed to cater to a separate water supply but normally one tap in the toilet will get unnecessarily blocked for this. This is just one not so humorous (for the sufferers at least!) example that gives one an idea of how shoddily the bureaucracy functions. It needs to be added that a DDG's (Brig.) office will not have an AC yet a Deputy Secretary's office will because Rule "Catch 22" applies. Of course, why recurring expenditure exists for a permanent need only a bureaucrat can volunteer to throw some light on. Any takers?

The concept of examinations originated in China and was started for the bureaucracy or the administrative service. Aspirants had to appear in the examination and secure 80% marks to be considered. Once enrolled in the service they had to appear in a similar examination once every two years and if they did not secure 70% marks they were out of service. It is high time the government introduced such measures that can boast of some sort of a specialization requirement for a particular ministry. All authority with no responsibility (or even accountability) hasn't exactly allowed for the emergence of an effective bureaucracy.

Since things have to be approved by bureaucrats or forwarded by them with positive comments, the armyman is forced to keep his smile perennially intact. Need one say more?

Olive Green Bureaucracy

While not drawing any punches aimed at the civilian bureaucracy one has to grudgingly admit that people in uniform, particularly in Headquarters, have a lot to learn as well. Since the concept of discipline is widely abused, senior officers at HQ get away with a lot that needs to be rectified. Ever so often one will find a general officer running to a junior bureaucrat's office because approval for one thing or the other has not come through and his boss (a three-star general) is putting him under duress. The civilian bureaucracy knows the uniformed bureaucracy only too well and likes paying games - therefore, trips abroad get approved at the last moment (though why some senior officers don't forgo the trip and make an issue of it is hard to fathom). On a more serious note, one is told that while the United Nations had paid the dues, our Indian bureaucracy could not ensure its payment to our first contingent that went to Cambodia. This has left nightmarish memories for the people involved.

A lot of this takes place simply because the Indian Army has no method to "grow" officers to fit into such ranks and appointments. Career advancement is so dependent on course gradings, appointments held and good ACRs (Annual Confidential Reports) that most of the people who successfully negotiate the obstacle course of promotions lack foresight, objectivity, independence, knowledge and the tactical acumen to negotiate threats posed by the civilian bureaucracy in particular and politics in general.

They (senior Army officer) bring with them the impatience of command (which is good at junior levels) and, supported by the disciplinary code, play havoc with the system. The result? Junior officers can hardly learn the right way to function. The vicious cycle goes on. Since tenure-based working is in vogue, personality orientation is very prominent. Everyone wants to boast about what he has achieved during his tenure. Reason? No one will take notice of what he has done for long-term good and therefore, he may miss the boat for the next rank or appointment. So, the OG bureaucracy does not lag far behind in creating obstacles to progress - but here it is for itself.

Roundup

Absurdities are likely to abound in such an environment. Take the case of Ordnance Factories - they had a captive market in the forces, especially the Army; they produced what they could and the expenditure was just adjusted to the cost (all book transactions anyway. Therefore, the Indian Army continues to use inefficient and expensive vehicles. Things have undergone some changes in recent times. R&D work 9 to 5 jobs and so only exceptions can make news (like the missile project). A ridiculous example that showcases just how out of date things continue to be is the fact that infantryman still use the raincoat that was in use during World War II (because R&D is still in the process of creating better raincoats)!

The problems are further propounded by not allowing the academic or corporate world or the judiciary to become knowledgeable so that they can also effectively contribute. But a convenient curtain called "national security" is hurriedly drawn across failures. No one is looking for genuine talent to participate in thinking and decision-making because we are hidebound by established structures. Organisation Analysis, Organisation Development, SWOT analysis, Cost Benefit Analysis and the like have never been given serious thought. A few in-house half-baked attempts and colourful presentations are made every now and then (by people who are very busy in their own jobs) but there is no sign of any visible movement as yet.

Other Countries

A brief look at the structure in other countries will be an indication of approaches to and the philosophy of defence planning elsewhere.

USA: Armed Forces Policy Council, Secretary of Defence and Joint Secretaries are at the Department of Defence level. All the departments come directly under the Department of Defence; one such department is the Army which has a Secretary and then Chief. The Chief is on hand for all briefings regarding the Army. This thereby ensures intimate interaction with the government.

China: National Defence Council advises the Council of Ministers. PLA (People Liberation Army as the Chinese Army is called) directly controls all else like ordnance depots, factories etc.

Germany: The defence minister has a sort of parallel relation with everyone including the Chief of Staff, Armed Forces and the respective Chiefs. Integration, therefore, is easy and effective.

Japan: The cabinet is advised by a National Defence Council. All Chiefs come directly under the Minister of State (Defence). Theoretically Japan does not have an Army - she has SDF (Self Defence Forces).

4

Time for Disinvestment

(Looking at Redundancies)

The Indian Army and organisations (like the MOD, R&D, Ordnance Factories etc) that claim to support it and look after it have continued to grow in number and very little has ever been done to seriously deconstruct or reconstruct. Despite great advancements in management concepts and processes and having four management institutes to support it, the Army and its linked organisations have done precious little to structurally upgrade itself. Of course, the danger of going overboard with changes has to be carefully monitored.

This kind of confusion takes place from time to time when committees are formed (headed by and composed of members who are not "suitable" for such a job) that submit reports which either gather dust or are implemented by "selective choice" (thereby increasing the confusion) or become a bargaining counter. A few examples are:

* A 400-page report was prepared on "reduction of paper work" but this has only served the purpose of increasing it even further. A very good policy was laid down - no new report/return could be introduced unless it fulfilled two criteria. One, it had to be fully justified before introduction. Two, some report/return had to be

dropped. But what actually happens is that units and HQ are initiating monthly, quarterly, half-yearly and annual reports on the same subject. If one generates so much of rubbish it is easy to employ a lot of people to clear it.

* A few years ago a study was carried out on the impact of changing the age of retirement. Yet when the decision was thrust on the Army (as was the case with others) it was "stumped".

* Training for counter insurgency is the need of the hour. Operational commands want at least doubling of their present capacity. But the "committee" is of the opinion that the institution is redundant and therefore should be done away with.

* During one of his visits to the UK, one defence secretary picked up a paper on "civilianisation" to cut down costs and wanted the same to be applied to the Indian Army. Absurd as it was, people had to waste time in analysing the paper, writing their comments and coming up with a fresh paper - after all, it had come from the "defence secretary". Coincidentally, around the same time a request was received from the head of a civilian defence organisation who was willing to trade in a dozen civilian workers for a single man in uniform.

Where is the sense in having institutions like the College of Defence Management, Defence Institute of Work Study, College of Materials Management (with the Management School), National Institute of Management (Calcutta), College of Combat, National Defence College etc if the Army fails to utilise the skills and talents available in these institutions. This is not to say that talent is not available in units and formations but people here are very busy with ground-level work. Decision making will neither be easy nor quick but once a plan and schedule are put into place the organisation will benefit greatly both in savings and in increasing effectiveness. Therefore, a study team (with members carefully selected for their objectivity, vision, analytical skills and the capacity to call a spade a spade irrespective of the toes crushed) with broad parameters and reasonable time (say a two-year frame) needs to be set up. Once the study is presented and decisions made a five-year plan has to be clearly laid out so that progress can be monitored. This study team should carefully analyse as to whether the organisation under its scrutiny is at all required. Is all the personnel needed, are all the departments in order, and are all the levels required and can the job be done by someone else or does it need to be done at all? Unfortunately, most people (in the government and in the forces) do not want to accept that every organisation exists to fulfil a need that lies outside their jurisdiction. The study team at all times must question ad nauseam, "if you do not exist, what happens then?" And, if the answer is vague, the organisation, department, appointment can be quite simply scrapped. Logically explained in the domestic context - a common sight in many households is a pile of junk gathering dust in a corner - cards, wire, bottles, papers etc. Not wanting to throw it out one is perpetually saying, "it could come in use later". If something has not been needed for over a year surely one can sell it to the junk dealer. The same logic applies here.

The study team's first job would be identification of organisations that definitely need to be studied (with "should" and "could" study categories). To assist such a study team, given below are: one, a suggested study team composition; and, two, a list of organisations that should be scrutinised for restructuring.

Study Team **(Will vary for other services).**

Chairman -A retired general who is known for his intelligence, farsightedness, objectivity and someone who is truly dedicated to the Army.

Deputy Chairman - A senior staff officer with similar qualities.

Members -*Four to six Army officers* (including two who have been in service less than 5 years - it is their army that is in question).

An academic (preferably someone who has specialised in international studies or economics).

One or two women (could even be those who have the skills needed in the team).

At least one *operations research expert* (application not theory).

Three or four *computer literate people* including programmers.

Systems analysts, inventory experts, project management experts.

Devil's advocate (introduce specially or enrol from the beginning).

Financial expert (including budgets).

Organisations

This list is nowhere near comprehensive. As the team views each part/department through a magnifying glass, it will be able to determine which is redundant and which crucial. Objectivity demands that each part be examined without any bias or preconceived notions. The whole exercise will be one in futility if a single link, level or personality (appointment) is overlooked. For instance, the MOD is rather likely to say it cannot come under the scrutiny of such a study - then there is no point in conducting the analysis because the study is for the nation and "empire" protection or special status is unacceptable.

1. **Ordnance Factories:** The availability of a captive market ensures lack of progress and competitiveness.

2. **Quality Assurance:** With the advent of ISOs and if one ensures warranty and guarantee there may be no need to have a separate organisation.

3. **Military Engineering Services:** In the late '60s, the MES said it was not possible to construct married accommodation in a particular area because their contractors would not be willing to work there. The Border Roads took up the challenge and built the accommodation (arguably the best married accommodation of the Army). Thought should have been given even then on reducing the MES stranglehold. A service that ends up spending more on its upkeep and less on servicing the clients' needs is no kind of service at all. In all such organisations (the study team must note), the ready excuse is that laid down policy or rules or directions are being followed. Where can one get a toilet made in the hills with local construction material for Rs 3,000? The MES estimate is Rs 24,000 (the ratio may have changed now). While the whole episode was possibly hushed up, one hears that the then Commandant of the College of Combat was moved out prematurely about a decade ago perhaps because he was ordering inquiries into the poor construction. The general, I am sure, would be able to throw more light on the subject. The MES would take up a couple of volumes so it would be up to the study team to take on. Contracting out seems a viable option.

4. R&D: The missile project is an unqualified success possibly because of certain individuals and some brilliant project management. Unfortunately, this does not hold true for most other establishments. Contributions of establishments must be carefully scrutinised and their shutting down, if so required, ought to be done totally objectively.

5. Committees: Committees that are either permanent or periodically set up must submit "cost-achievement" analyses. Take the "Hindi Implementation Committee" - its relevance is debatable in the Army's context where the lingua franca is Hindi anyway. Correspondence (including orders) is in the convenient language for the subject: English or Hindi. Primarily, it does not need monitoring and second, it does not need a team to travel to all parts of the country at government expense anyway. Anyhow, other committees may not be doing things very much different.

6. Army Welfare Housing Organisation (AWHO): At the prices this organisation sells flats the word "welfare" should be removed from its title immediately. It needs to be analysed whether the AWHO need exist at all. There are a number of viable alternatives especially when the armyman keeps paying in advance as the construction work goes on and there is no protection against escalation. Even the quality of construction when compared to many others in the business is highly questionable. Once again the question of establishment comes up.

7. National Cadet Corps: The NCC as an organisation has great potential to help the young even though it is able to touch only about 3% of the total student population. All the three services contribute personnel, equipment and assistance to the NCC. It is an organisation that can be easily exploited for limelight activities. The organisation, thanks to their head, conducted the "national games" in 1997 and 1998 that cost a great deal. This was at the expense of the Centre and states. Genuine achievement? A prominent "Zero". Students barely get enough time to carry out basic NCC activities; and games and sports have never been a part of NCC curricula. Massive PR exercise has ensured that no major criticism is levelled against anyone in particular. Consequently, the media has effectively been fooled. The so-called "competitive" spirit ensured irregularities (cadets on paper for the games); after all you can't create sportsmen overnight. Even the "Permit Meet" did not draw spectators but compulsory attendance and displays (states) tried to occupy the stands. In very many places there is no administrative support and NCOs travel 70-80 kms by bus to take classes. In addition senior NCOs are misused as runners, sometimes even to cut grass! There is no need for a heavy central organisation because the actual work is done at unit level - where all support is needed. Since the Navy and Air Force do none of the menial work and the armyman is too disciplined (and polite) to refuse, its men are kept running from pillar to post. The Army should not look at the NCC only because a substantial number of officers, JCOs and NCOs can be placed: if the Army can do without them they need to look for alternatives to get them off the Army's strength. Because of warped priorities the NCC has lost its focus and concentrates today only on the Republic Day Camp and the mockery of the Independence Day camp for games. It is required to trim the structure and concentrate on units (which are actually in touch with schools, colleges and cadets); the central organisation is needed only for coordination. One must reiterate that the amount of good the NCC as an ethos can do for young people must not be lost sight of but it desperately needs overhauling. A single person should not be allowed to mess up the entire focus.

8. MOD: This organisation should have headed the list because a basic lack of understanding, absence of will and lack of positive attitude – all these contribute to tremendous losses at the MOD, not to mention delays and frustration. Analyses must include "authority -- accountability", "level of absurdity", "delay and frustration potential", "level of arrogance", "exchange potential" ((quid pro quo - or what do I get in return) and many others. Misuse of authority - a case that could be analysed in detail (quite widely written about in the media) is of a general officer being given an extension (against all norms) and then being promoted (though he was not approved for such a promotion). While studying the MOD and its innumerable tentacles, brooms of all shapes and sizes will be required for the clean up operation.

9. Army: Needless to say, the whole structure of the Army needs a critical study beginning with the Army Headquarters and then moving further down the ladder. Redundancies of appointments and staff, organisation will inevitably show up. Dual and triple controls, too many approvals, too much paper work, absurd rules and regulations, archaic rules etc will surface without having to dig too deep. Still, one is tempted to focus on a few areas:-

AEC — Army Education Corps is perhaps the one fully redundant organisation. Recruitment in most cases is now at matriculation level so the AEC's job is rendered redundant anyway. As far as map reading is concerned no commander relies on the AEC - he trains his own people. Desperate to cling on to something, all kinds of gimmicks (like language courses, music courses, etc and Human Resource Development Centres or HRDC - which do anything but

HRD - new examinations and so on) have been invented by them.

EME — Whatever be the justification, one cannot accept a maintenance service having a strength larger than that of the mechanised forces.

Training Centres — Optimal usage of facilities, instructors and personnel needs looking into.

Word of Caution

It must, however, be realised that certain aspects are best left to the Army. It has been mentioned earlier the danger of going overboard ostensibly under the cover of "change" - a few years ago we were witness to a defence minister who wanted to sell off prime land; and who gave all kinds of reasons and excuses for this endeavour. Pitfalls such as these have to be guarded against. Real estate in the Army's possession is well taken care of and it is in the country's best interest that status quo be maintained. It is not without any effort that cantonments and other areas, within the jurisdiction of the Army, look so well maintained. The bottom-line? Make things that are already satisfactory even better and do not make changes simply for the sake of change. However, do not hesitate to apply the knife to the fatty and infected portions.

Courage must be shown in accepting cost-benefit analyses, developmental changes and so on. In my 32 years of Army life, I have not seen the lives of troops touched by Defence R&D and therefore the feelings can be appreciated.

5

How Do You Spend Your Time?

An often asked question by people who have not been exposed to an Army routine (or have forgotten their experience when attached to units - like the IAS, IA & AS, IPS, IFS etc) is "how do you spend your time"? What an army person does is greatly dependent on where he/she is posted and to a lesser extent on who the boss is. Different arms and services, because of their typical work content, would necessarily have different routines.

Here, a routine that would be generally applicable is given:

Reveille-0500 hrs

PT-0600-0645 hrs

Training-0800-1230 hrs

Lunch-1300-1345 hrs

Leisure-1345-1500 hrs

Getting the area into shape-1500-1600 hrs

Games-1615-1800 hrs

Roll Call-1830 hrs

Dinner-1900-2000 hrs

Leisure & Preparation-2000-2200 hrs

Lights out-2200 hrs

To this apparently simple routine one has to add the following:-

* Drawing of weapons from Kotes.
* Cleaning the weapons and returning them to kote.
* Washing of clothes, polishing of boots, belts and other items.
* Education and other classes for those preparing for examinations.
* Preparing instructional material - instructors as also people attending cadres and being trained to become instructors.
* Personnel for various duties including looking after the Quarter Guard (the pride of the unit).

Saturdays are normally utilised for Drill and weekly maintenance as also documentation.

Sundays, in most units, start with a visit to the place of worship. In the Indian Army, for officers, a practice that is in vogue is "your troop's religion is yours" so on Sundays it is not at all uncommon to see a Christian officer going to the mandir and later visiting the church. Given the rural background of a large (overwhelming) percentage of people religion plays an important role in the armyman's life. In the business he is in faith is an important factor. In a number of units in the Army a unique concept is followed, that of a single place of worship for all religions. This is done without sacrificing or compromising on the sanctity of any religion. This has been in vogue for quite some time now and has proved very successful.

The routine changes quite considerably in field areas where forward defended localities (FDLs) have to be manned along the line of control or in high altitude (or super high altitude). Operational duties, maintenance of defence works, dealing with firing from across the border etc is added on to the base routine. Which is essential to keep everyone fit in all respects. Training cadres, preparing for courses and so on continue meanwhile. However, in counter insurgency areas the operational load is so intense that part of the routine has to be sacrificed. Life becomes quite intense because of the unpredictability, sustained operations and the pressure to show results.

For some of the combat and supporting arms, a few camps are very important due to availability of suitable training and firing facilities. The engineers, for example, have to focus on their "bridging training camp (BTC)" and "combat engineering training camp"; the artillery on their "practice camps"; the signals on their "technical camps"; the armoured corps on their "field firing" and so on.

To all the above one has to add VIP visits, Sand Model discussions, war games, tactical exercises without troops, conducting camps for children, planting of trees, conducting ex-servicemen's rallies, school functions, Battle Honour/ Raising Day celebrations and other such events. When formation exercises are on, though the schedule is busy, all other activities get pushed into the background.

The fact is that whenever one sees a unit appearing neat and clean or a function taking off like clockwork one perhaps does not give much thought to the immense amount of planning and preparation that goes into it prior to the event.

But Murphy's Law applies even in the Army - a dog will run through the drill square just as the ceremonial parade is on - while saluting (too) smartly a cap will get knocked off - the stove (in high altitude) will refuse to work just as the visitor readies himself for a cup of tea - the waiter will drop something on the chief guest during a ceremonial dinner........... Hiccups like these, however are all taken in one's stride and after the event are remembered almost with fondness.

For the officers the routine is always extended, following Chetewode's motto. Also, individual activities for career development have to continue. In addition, they have to find additional time for games that are not considered troop games. To be a professional and earn the respect of his command an officer has to do much more than survive a routine.

6

Training

Unlike the IAS, IPS and IFS where a posting to a training establishment is considered infra dig by people who feel they have been sidelined (and desperately try to get out), it is considered a great privilege in the Army. First, one has to qualify in the relevant courses, get a good grading and be recommended to be an instructor. Second, out of the lot of similarly qualified officers/JCOs/NCOs one must make it on merit though certain other aspects like availability, other courses planned etc, also are taken into account. Third, all training institutions can send a person back if he/she is not found suitable in the first three months.

Therefore, even from the career point of view training is important. But to enable a person to face a war situation training becomes critical. "The more you sweat in peace the less you bleed in war" is a poignant maxim. One may term the Army's training as "graduated" and sometimes "assignment oriented". The professional approach, openness and experiential orientation always impress a number of foreign officers (and sometimes NCOs) who train in our schools of instruction. Sometimes, they (especially those coming from western countries) cannot fathom why there is a lack of helicopters and other such backup. They also cannot understand why a professional Army like ours lacks basic equipment like sniper rifles, door openers or lightweight bullet proof jackets or why the change over from 7.62 mm rifles is so sluggish (especially when the Indian Army had first thought of the need to go in for a lower calibre 5.56mm or 5.65 mm as early as 1948/49).

Process

Progressive training ensures competence building and also prepares people for various appointments the person will be holding later. A general flow would appear something like this:-

OTHER RANKS	OFFICERS
Training Centres	RIMC/Military/Sainik Schools
Unit Orientation	NDA,OTA,IMA (All round)
Skills/Trades Training	Young Officers' Courses
Operations Orientation Training (Periodic)	Unit Cadres, Other Courses
Promotion/Upgradation Cadres	Promotion Examinations
Specific Skills Courses e.g.	81mm Mortar Course
Technical Degree Courses/	Specialisation Courses
Training in units (Continuous)	Junior Command Course
More Specific Courses	Promotion Examinations
Promotion/Upgradation	Competitive Examination & Selection: Staff College
Orientation Training (Role/ Location change)	By Selection: Senior Command/Long Courses

Contd.

Continued.

Tactical/Leadership Courses	By Selection: Higher Command/Long Defence Management Course
Promotion to JCO cadre	By Selection: National Defence College
Pre-retirement Courses	

Note: Some courses abroad may come at any level.

Training is a continuous process in units; Sand model discussions, exercise (with or without troops), war games etc.

In actuality, the training calendar is always full in the Army. In addition to the broad outline given above there are:

* Physical Training (PT) Tests
* Battle Physical Efficiency Tests (BPET)
* Physical Proficiency Tests (PPT)
* Firing and weapon training
* Navigation
* Endurance training
* Field craft
* Explosives and mines training
* Technical training (for the technical arms and services)
* Technical camps
* Exercises at platoon level and upwards
* Patrolling
* Camouflage

* Communications
* Presentations
* Seminars
* Study fortnights
* Training programmes outside the Army
* Mountains and High Altitude Training
* Drill
* Watermanship
* Varied terrain training
* Parachute training (for Parachute Regiment, Special Forces and personnel in support of such forces) and more.

For the officers, training has to spill over to the sports and social field. Sports because he/she must have the capacity to supervise and play because it is required to rub shoulders with the troops under command. Social field because after all an officer is a gentleman first.

Computer training is also widely applicable because of greater automation and increased use of computers for various activities. Taking a step ahead one also has to be familiar with "simulations". Wide exposure is provided to all Army personnel so that awareness is at its highest possible - be it in the field of environment or historical monuments or languages.

Unfortunately, one thing they are not taught is "how to blow one's own trumpet".

Institutions

There is a large number of training establishments that cater to all kinds of training: basic at the training centres and subsequently at specialist schools of each arm/service. There are a few training establishments that are combined (all arms and services) or are inter-service (Army, Navy, Air Force). To give the reader some idea about these a list is given below:

* The Infantry School.
* Armoured Corps Centre and School.
* School of Artillery.
* Air Defence and Guided Missile School.
* College of Military Engineering (CME).
* Military College of Telecommunication Engineering (MCTE).
* Army Service Corps School (ASC School).
* College of Materials Management (CMM).
* Armed Forces Medical College (AFMC).
* Military College of Electrical and Mechanical Engineering (MCEME).
* Army School of Mechanical Transport (ASMT).
* College of Combat.
* Military Intelligence School and Depot (MINTSD).
* Corps of Military Police School (CMP School).
* Counter Insurgency and Jungle Warfare School (CIJWS).

* Parachute Training School.(PTS)
* Defence Services Staff College (DSSC).
* Institute of Armament Technology (IAT).
* College of Defence Management (CDM).
* National Defence College (NDC).
* Army Education Corps School and Centre.
* Institute of National Integration (INI). This is a unique institution that trains selected personnel to be religious teachers. Religious teachers are all trained in the four main religions. They also conduct National Integration courses for all arms and services.
* High Altitude Warfare School (HAWS).
* Army Medical Corps School (AMC School).

There are some institutions like the Mountaineering Institutions that are supported by the Army (and MOD).

Cross training between arms and services as also with the Navy and Air Force are planned and encouraged. For a few years now, officers from the combat arms (after due selection) are being encouraged to take up technical degree courses.

Publications

To assist training processes and to ensure uniformity there are a number of training publications that are published by the Army and periodically reviewed. Sometimes these publications get fairly dated because they are required to be printed at government presses with their linked inefficiency and time overruns. Often, publications see the light of day more than a year after they should have been out. Once again, the problem of a captive market crops up.

There are basic publications on operations of war, administration and so on; on an as-required basis Training Memorandums are also published. At the formation level Training Notes are also issued. It would not be incorrect to state that whatever the subject there will always be reference material that is easily available. Sometimes the "need to know" rule has to be applied in the case of certain publications.

In addition to the above, most training establishments publish their own journals which cover a wide variety of subjects. These are current and thought provoking. Some autonomous bodies like the United Services Institution of India (popularly known as the USI) also produce very readable and professional pieces. The USI, incidentally, also conducts correspondence courses for promotion examinations and Staff College (competitive entrance examination). The USI's library also enjoys an excellent reputation. Institute for Defence Studies and Analysis (IDSA) publishes a number of booklets that are quite useful to students of war and the military.

For specific information the most appropriate publication can be contacted for details.

Roundup

Training is a major impact area for the Army and a lot of details are continuously being linked and addressed. No other organisation takes such comprehensive care to train its members. Yet, sometimes, one does feel that much more time is spent than is necessary because of poor planning (and lack of concern for others). Most exercises take place in summer and people take great pride in being out for two to three months though a fortnight may produce better results - but as I said, "who cares"?

For battle inoculation and field firing, some nominated ranges are used. Battle noises and some semblance of dust etc creates a reasonably realistic picture. But then again, it is not "war" - unpredictability cannot be built in and safety regulations do not permit the shaking up as would be normal. The Army does try, however, to make all such training as close to the real picture as is possible.

7

The Feeble Handshake

(Preparing for Retirement)

The young village boy attends a recruiting rally and is thoroughly impressed with the charts, posters and men dressed in olive green uniforms. So, he decides to give it a try. Being physically fit, he goes through the tests quite easily. Medically too he is declared to be in sound health. Next, he clears the written exam and gets a call letter. He joins a training centre - he is all of 16 years old. Ten months of rigorous training later, he steps forward as a soldier; 17 years (which includes the training period) later - if he has failed to get a promotion - he retires at the ripe "old" age of 33 without a clue as to what he ought to do next. All the talk (and papers and posters) of the Army and MOD regarding resettlement of retired personnel is filled with hot air for most people and for most of the time. Not trained in the art of bribing, which sadly to say comes quite easily to a major portion of people who live on the "civi street", he is unable to fit into any of the so-called quotas. True, some people do make it to "nice" jobs (they often become security officers where the pay isn't too bad). But for one, the members are too few to be counted as a big deal and secondly, the job profile is rather poor. The rest either land up as security guards with a measly pay of Rs 2,000 rupees a month or simply stay at home wishing they could get decent jobs.

The retired young man has skills which are highly specific to the Army - it is an employers' market – but the turnover in the numbers is far greater than the number of available jobs. Self-discipline is perhaps the only thing that keeps him away from becoming a mercenary or less. Certainly he thinks (rues) of all the hardships he has faced, all the sacrifices his family has made, but to his credit - he is immensely more mature than the Indian politician - he does not openly protest nor does he switch loyalties. The values he has imbibed during his career in the Army is perhaps the only thing that props him up.

Some years back, a friend of mine who works for the United Nations on projects in rural areas happened to ask me, "How does the Army change a person so much?" He cited the example of two brothers from a village, one of who went off to join the Army. My friend kept going back to the village and worked with the brother who had stayed behind. During one of his visits about three years later the brother in the Army also happened to be home on leave and lent a helping had to the project. It was then he said to me that "I realised I was dealing with a totally different person - self confident, quick on the uptake, offering alternatives, enjoying the work". Until my friend brought this to my notice I had never given the matter any serious thought. This change in personality takes place because of a number of reasons:

* Training

* Inter-dependence in order to succeed.

* The need to do things right the very first time. (There are no second chances during an armed conflict).

* Importance of being part of a whole.
* Working independently.
* Working on the basis of aims and objectives.
* Exposure to all kinds of people, varying environments and separate thoughts.
* Imbibing new values.

Here was a civilian who despite his limited exposure to the Army had clearly noticed the distinction yet our august nation - the government and its organs essentially – fail to acknowledge the quality of the Army jawan and lets him waste away from the age of 33/34 onwards. This is nothing short of a national disgrace – to take the best years of his life and then to simply forget about him. This is of course provided he is not already dead having become a martyr in an armed conflict while defending the nation in the line of duty.

What most people fail to realise is that the outgoing personnel can easily be put to work in trickles across all central and state government organisations and undertakings. If corporate houses and the industry act sensibly they will be the ultimate beneficiaries. In this way, it is possible for every single person to have an extended (albeit second) career. His pension and other dues (when he retires) must stay protected as a mark of national gratitude for his service. Everyone is aware of the fact that such an arrangement is a totally viable one but one will be forced to question as to what will happen to the "exchange" value and extra earnings? This is an issue that has to be resolved by the government and the nation. It simply will not do to push such a large number of trained people into a state of mass frustration.

While still in service, there is simply no time for the armyman to plan for retirement. In fact, a defence secretary has gone on record to say that he must concentrate on his job and not get diverted to post retirement prospects - and the Army top brass (like a bunch of fools) has let it pass. Prior to retirement, there are a few courses offered by the Resettlement Directorate but they are too few to be of any real import. A career in the Army career implies a high degree of "specificity" and therefore, long-term plans and training have to be worked out.

What happens to the officers? Through a competitive examination – a select lot go for the SSB (Services Selection Board) – a few people are selected and go through a medical board. According to merit they are detailed to join the Academy for which they have applied - the NDA, IMA or OTA. Everyone trains for the scheduled period (NDA entry - 4 years, IMA – one to one-and-a-half years, OTA - 10 months) and pass out as officers (a number of them, to ensure proper training, have to repeat terms or appear in retests etc). Once commissioned they have to undergo certain mandatory courses and pass promotion examinations to pick up their ranks. In addition, officers invariably take up more courses to further their knowledge as well as to increase their prospects. For the Defence Services Staff College (course) they have to pass a tough entrance examination (which is an open competition) and make it to the merit list (as per vacancies); the course is of almost a year's duration. For the technical streams, except for the technical graduate entry, an engineering course has to be successfully completed. From Maj. to Lt. Col., officers are promoted only after having been screened by a selection board - this holds true for all ranks beyond. Needless to say, the numbers that are approved for promotion are roughly related to the number of vacancies.

Therefore the hierarchical pyramid has to declare "unfit" a significant number of perfectly fit people. If they are given openings in other government sectors then everybody benefits. But shortsighted decision-makers have two responses to this. The civilian one being "why should we absorb these people"? And the Army's - a dog in the manger attitude – "we will be short of officers at junior levels". If the Army can't offer a full and satisfying career in uniform to people, other ways must be found in order to extend their careers instead of hanging on to them for purely selfish reasons.

The Army should allow anyone who wants to leave (except for a certain mandatory period that can be sensibly laid down for initial service for appointments and special courses done at the expense of the government) the option to do so. An organisation like the Army must have the resilience to handle such departures. After all, the armyman could be an asset to the civilian world and if he does well, the Army can pat itself itself on the back – after all wasn't it the army regimen that made him what he is today?

The changeover from Maj. to Lt. Col. takes place when officers are around 35 years old - a reasonable enough age to take on a second career. Instead of encouraging these people to think of the prospects beyond the Army, it tends to hang on to officers to keep the numbers intact. Finally when they do leave, the officers (in most cases) are too old to be able to begin a second career.

Severance is what the officer gets - the Army plays no part in providing a better deal. The civil government makes matters even worse. Very little, if any, training is provided to the Army officers to fit into careers outside. The Army exhorts everyone to be good regimental soldiers, which sadly makes them almost unfit for the civilian world. The final handshake, therefore, lacks warmth and concern.

This status needs to be rectified at the earliest possible. Why does such a situation have to prevail at all? The non uniform attitude goes like this: "They may perform better - in any case, why should we share the cake?" while the Army's is to point out that senior officers who are the decision makers are not affected and are too scared to thump the table anyway. They align to that vapour of a hope that they may land a plum appointment. The bottom-line is that the armyman is the loser when he has to hang up his uniform.

Periodically (and regularly) the Army has to shed people at every selection rank - in effect, this implies that well qualified and well-adjusted officers become unsuitable overnight. To make matters worse this is conveyed in an arrogant, harsh and unfeeling manner "......... you have not been approved for selection to........". If a complaint comes forward it is investigated without any proper discussion or analysis basically because it is done by people who either do not know the person concerned or have no idea about how things are at the working level. And, the reply is even worse – "..... no injustice has been done" - ironical, isn't it? The authorities can't claim "....... justice has been done". Credibility is completely lacking from the system. Does it come as any surprise then to find more and more people opting out of the Army? Disillusioned because they don't have the faintest idea as to why they were considered unsuitable for promotion. All because the Army does not even have the courage to tell its people why. In effect, the Army ruins the self-esteem of individuals in such cases. A small percentage does commence a second career but the bulk fade away or take up lesser jobs. This is exactly how the MOD would like it, and it would definitely suit the bureaucracy just fine. The problem, after all, is someone else's.

A complete mockery is made out of the entire situation when in some cases the people concerned are asked to send their resumes to the MOD to be considered for jobs in the civil sector. Since the Army officers themselves cannot apply directly (either individually or organisationally) the Catch 22 situation applies. The MOD circulates only those offers where there would be very good chances of no one qualifying and if someone's credentials do meet the laid down conditions, chances are that the application and resume will not go beyond the MOD. The bureaucracy and its members, after all, are all in it for some personal gains and hope to share some of the plum appointments.

The long and short of it is (in general practice) that the MOD, the government and the nation remember the Army only in times of a crisis and at superannuation time, conveniently forget those men in olive green.

If the armyman does not wish to be at the mercy of others, then as an organisation the Army must get its act together and ensure that all personnel are trained and prepared in the event of their having to leave the Army. Some areas worth looking into:-

* Continuous training.
* Possible internships spread over their career span.
* Aptitude testing.
* Deal directly with other departments, industry etc.
* Hold interactive seminars and workshops with industry, government departments, PSUs etc. Allow others to see Army personnel for themselves and gauge their worth.

* Prepare them for the change.
* Provide effective financial advice.
* Set up and run profitable industries/organisations.
* Take direct contracts for manpower.
* Act as a proper placement agency.

The decision-makers have to only seriously try: currently they are simply "busy being busy".

While the bureaucracy continues to manipulate and manoeuvre since the politicians have never taken interest anyway, it falls squarely on the shoulders of the Army top brass to get a move on and do something about the sad state of affairs. They have sat on their high chairs for so long and have done enough empty talking at meetings (which should in any case be attended by 2 or 3 levels junior) that it's time they put forward a long-term plan and implemented it. If in the process some bureaucratic and political toes are trod upon, so be it.

Resettlement or adjustment in a fresh career is very much the responsibility of the nation so far as the Army (and the other defence services) is concerned. Especially the Army because its personnel are rarely, if ever, located at places (where they can look at other avenues) for a reasonable period of time. It is also important to remember that the skills learnt are really useful only in the Army (whereas Naval and Air Force personnel can shift to similar civil organisations). An option that could be seriously considered is to offer the armyman's services directly to other countries, large corporate organisations of the world, even large NGOs. If this means letting people go at a younger age (permanently or on tenures) the Army must accept it. Enough rubbish is mouthed by the top brass about "...... we have invested in their training........." or "we will run short of manpower" and so on. A few points need to be driven home. One, unit commanders are the only ones (if anyone is) genuinely interested in the resettlement of their troops. Two, training to troops is provided only by unit commanders (and on courses), therefore the senior officers' views are irrelevant. Three, units can always handle a slightly larger turnover. Four, such a flow will create an environment enabling people to perform better. Five, thanks to poor policies and even poorer implementation, employment will always (till the distant future at least) remain a problem in India therefore, and ironically so, the recruitment base will always be fairly good.

Regimental centres, where the troops (JCOs and other ranks) spend almost a month before proceeding on pension do precious little to help these people. Centres seem to be more busy running commercial ventures or ceremonials. While training is certainly the most important duty of these centres surely resettlement is no less so. To emhasise my point, I'd like to cite a personal experience. Having called up one such centre and informed it of job openings (for drivers, supervisors, clerks etc) the response was as follows:

One: "We will put up a notice and interested people will call you back"; two: "Please tell the Depot Company commander - he deals with them"; three: "People are not really interested. "My efforts were purely with the purpose to help (I am sure there are others who pass on such offers). The attitude is upsetting though one is still willing to take calls directly from JCOs/NCOs, give them contact addresses, telephone members, job descriptions etc and hope they will find good jobs.

Centre Commandants must take it upon themselves to do a lot more than what they are already doing. A few suggestions:-

* As an organisation increase communications with corporate houses, industry, individuals who can employ, NGOs etc so that a steady flow can start.

* Provide genuine training to become entrepreneurs and keep in touch with organisations that can help like Bhartiya Yuva Shakti Trust etc.

* Keep in touch with organisations like CII, FICCI, Chambers of Commerce, small scale industries development, state governments etc. (The Adjutant General should be doing this at the macro level all the time. Since no results have been visible so far, because of lack of concern or vision perhaps, centre commandants need to take up the gauntlet individually. After all, these JCOs/NCOs depend on them).

* Invest in small-scale industries which can absorb some people, provide training and also earn some money for the Centre to be spent on welfare, sports etc. Printing press, contract for coolers in Army offices, sports goods manufacture etc would be worth considering.

* Transport companies.

There is an urgent need for concern and commitment to provide retiring Army personnel with some sort of back up to enable them to earn adequately. One needs to ensure that retired personnel commit themselves and have a degree of ownership in any of these ventures. The underlying philosophy must be "helping them to help themselves" or "facilitating growth". Needless to add, those sitting on the topmost rungs of the hierarchical ladder in the Army must do more. Talking less, giving fewer speeches and having a smaller number of committees would be an added advantage! The armyman must remember hanging up his uniform fondly.

NOTE

The Indian Army could take a leaf out of our neighbour's book. The Pakistan Army runs a very large number of industries through retired personnel. Along with the other two defence services, their holdings are only less than the largest corporate house in Pakistan. Point to ponder, isn't it?

8

With Due Respect

(Lack of Knowledge about the Army)

Saying "I don't know" or "Could you please explain" or "I am not the right person to give an opinion" - takes a lot of courage. The courage to be honest is an uncommon virtue in society at large. In the process a lot gets done (that should not be done) or remains undone (that should be done).

Looking Inwards

Army officers, as they grow in service and rank (very often) forget to evolve themselves as much as they need to. They fail to update their views and knowledge - with the result the Army is not as forward looking as it should be. General officers still waste time sighting light machine guns, holding weekly (some hold morning conferences daily) conferences, seeking more and more data. The bottom-line is that a very large number of senior officers refuse to introspect objectively, they constantly transgress to their (now totally irrelevant) times. At times they avoid even a healthy dissent shovelling it into the pit as "conflict and confrontation". They are so "tenure" oriented that a very large number of them spend their terms on short-sighted projects in order to "show" their work. Sometimes these multiple standards are sickening but people get away with them because of the following:-

* The Army Act acts as the Sword of Damocles.
* Basic discipline.
* The innate goodness of the armyman.
* Annual Confidential Report.
* Juniors lack the moral courage to even politely protest.

When the Army is excluded from activities such as the decision making process or in the selection of the teams to go abroad or any other such matter, there is not even a murmur of protest from senior officers in Delhi. As a group it is not the best of examples to emulate. Take the mundane example of a Commanding Officer grading one of his men poorly simply because the Brigade Commander felt that officer "A" did not deserve a better report, even though the CO himself has no complaints against officer "A". The Army needs to inject a lot more of objectivity into its bloodstream and do away with all the sycophancy that it abounds in. One must hasten to add that this is not a new phenomenon lest the really senior officers think they are above all of this – the truth of it is that they are at the very nerve centre of this phenomenon.

One has to grant, however, that where civilian "controls" are concerned a stand taken by one officer (even the Chief) will not bear results - at least, six or seven officers need to voice their categorical objections. The distant promise of governorship shouldn't tempt them because (going by the government's track record) very few are going to make it anyway. Since the bureaucrat hardly ever retires, all the openings for chairmanship, heads of committees etc have to be kept open for them. It is no small annoyance then to see senior officers unable to catch the bull by the horns - their weakness becomes even more apparent when they look to only their subordinates to get their own dirty jobs done.

Senior officers in the Army obviously have one big failing - they think managing the internal environment is their job. They couldn't be further from the truth. In different doses, a senior officer's (from a Brigadier upwards at least) primary task is to manage and supervise the external environment - he has enough staff officers and subordinates to manage the internal environment. Unfortunately, he has not educated himself to do so and so he reverts to the familiar - what he does know. In this particular sphere the training is grossly inadequate (the Army does not send officers for development programmes that are appropriate. Even if one is rank bound (and not capability bound) the Army must send Brigs. and Maj. Gens. for programmes meant for CEOs. A Maj. Gen. upwards must attend global programmes and take short sabbaticals to understand the macro processes of the country.

Perhaps the so-called "civilian control" would not like Army officers to be exposed to such training but the Army must get the same for its senior officers.

Politicians

They are expected to guide and lead the nation forward. If they do not care to understand one of the instruments of policy, the Army, the politicians are just not nationalistic enough. As members of the parliament they are expected to evince more keen interest in the affairs of the nation - the Army plays an important role in this. Of course, the cabinet, defence minister and prime minister have a direct role to play in any activity related to the Army. But knowledge cannot be expected to emerge as an "Eureka" sort of experience. How then do our politicians acquire this knowledge? The nagging suspicion at the back of the mind is that not very many take any interest at all and there is no facility for formal acquisition of the required knowledge. So, ignorant as they may be, they strut about being pretenders to great knowledge and insight into the intricacies involved in the functioning of the Army. What could be more dangerous? A loaded gun in a monkey's hand? It is like a defence minister who feels he knows everything just because he has a retired Naik for a brother. The political arena: Army equation is quite striking: unionism on the one hand - discipline on the other, politics and manipulation on one hand and an apolitical organisation on the other, free speech on one hand and highly restricted freedom of expression on the other. The list is never ending. Since very few politicians and parliamentarians have much understanding of the Army they need to learn. To take major decisions that concern the Army is an immense responsibility the nation has placed with the politicians and parliamentarians. Within this group there are some (yet not enough) people who have earlier served in the Army. They can be utilised to form an advisory group. Even better would be to invite serving or retired officers/JCOs/NCOs from different levels (seniority and competence wise) to form the advisory body. Periodic briefing by the Chief, PSOs (Principal Staff Officers) would also go a long way in providing suggestions and help.

The Army is apolitical - so are its personnel. Still, thought is difficult to control in an information free world. The "politician" should not assume that the armyman does not think or is ill informed. The armyman is fully aware of the facts of a political leader's "normal" way of life. Like 48 suitcases of personal baggage of a provincial leader running

(!) desperately from corruption charges, about sprawling bungalows being converted into family heirlooms or "offices", about a couple of crores of rupees discovered in the puja room, about a prostrate government wanting to put a hundred crores (or more) into a trust/foundation, about the misuse of defence aircraft, about Swiss bank accounts and Bofors linkage, about government money being used to fund insurgents. This list is not exhaustive. It could fill a volume. But the point being made is that the armyman may not make any comments but he hears, reads, sees and perceives as well as anyone else. It may not be too long before he will pose the question, "Are our sacrifices worth putting these people into power?"

The politician needs to, or at least try to, bridge the credibility gap. Expecting them to be role models is like asking for the moon but they can try to be a little more transparent in their functioning. If politicians increase their knowledge, talk sense, work in the interests of the people, the armyman could condescend to accept them. It will not be easy to clamber out into the clearing (in credibility accounts) having been in the red since Independence but they can try. A word of advice. Do no hesitate to seek help - the Army is a complex institution and not knowing about it is understandable but not wanting to know is inexcusable. When parliament is in session officers are directed not to leave office till the session ends for the day. What the armyman thinks of this is best left unsaid.

Bureaucrats

Of course, there are exceptions to the rule but by and large the bureaucracy's sole interest lies in wielding power. This is transparent in their display of indifference and arrogance. One sometimes wonders if they are working for this country or if they are on the American president's planning team! Lack of honesty (and moral courage) is evident from the way files move to and from the bureaucracy (mainly the MOD in the Army's case) without anything concrete being achieved at the end of the exercise. Their already inflated egos are massaged by a number of people (mostly senior officers who are so keen to "get the job done" that in the process they completely upset the power equation).

The bureaucrat takes immense pleasure in delaying cases (as if it is a business contract) so that people hound him with requests to clear the case. In many instances the Army slips up because the senior officers wanted the job done "the day before yesterday" and adequate time is not spent on analysing the case. The other "in house" problem is that every senior officer wants to change what his predecessor had said. It is the staff officer's headache to change and play with language while sending the noting (giving the bureaucrat the openings he/she seeks).

Having been on the job (of delaying, laying obstacles, favouring and analysing exchange value) longer than necessary, the bureaucrat wins this battle hands down. Here are a few gems from their collection:-

* "Your Para 3 is not very clear, please forward a comprehensive Statement of Case."

* "The information relating to finances have not been included." When it is pointed out that in the same noting, under a separate heading 'Financial Implications', it has been stated that there is no expenditure involved, the reply will

come, "To enable us to process the case and forward the same to the RRM, a financial statement of case may be sent."

* Or a Joint Secretary will sign off a letter asking for a personal explanation of a DG (Director General with the rank of Lt. Gen.). Instead of sending the letter back and asking the bureaucrat to shove it wherever he likes– discipline being in his blood, the senior officer gets down to framing a reply. Of course, some senior officers ask subordinates (two down, at least) to sign the reply which isn't too bad a move.

* "This office agrees to the proposal in principle. Comments of the Ministry of Law is being sought". (After that they will send it to Ministry of External Affairs - meanwhile, the deadline will be over).

* "The case is returned herewith. Please resubmit along with three copies". Why they did not ask for the copies in the first place, only Chanakya knows.

Let it suffice to say that the bureaucracy, in general, is extremely poorly thought of. Virtually all the problems in this country are a direct outcome of the lack of foresight and pathetically poor administration. In both these fields the lead (and permanent) players are the bureaucrats. There are some retired bureaucrats who even have the gall to say that the Army has a stake in keeping insurgency alive - such a sweeping statement can only come from people who are not leaders in the true sense of the word. People who don't give a damn about how many lives are lost due to insurgent operations. Bureaucrats are not relationship oriented - they are self-centred. No wonder the Army and the bureaucracy can't get along - for the Army thinks in terms of an extended family and anyone injured or wounded or killed is a brother. At a book release (Overcoming Crisis in Leadership: Indian

Army) an eminent journalist said, "...... the long and short of it is that the Defence Secretary does not play golf with any of the Chiefs". The statement was packed with meaning but hardly anyone made a note of it (the Raksha Mantri was present) and this was long before the unsavoury "Admiral Bhagwat" episode.

Bureaucrats have to get off their high horses and must be put through a proper orientation course before they are allowed to take up any appointment in the MOD. If found unsuitable they should simply be transferred to another department.

Academics

Academics and teachers have strong opinions and form biases which inevitably get passed onto a large number of young people. Most are good rhetoricians and begin with the added advantage of the young crowd looking up to them. It is therefore crucial for academics and teachers to realise exactly what kind of information they are passing on to their students. Great discretion needs to be exercised in this regard. Where there are loopholes in their knowledge and theory, they need to work on it to bridge the gap between opinion and fact. After all, it is not an uncommon sight to see the lack of complete knowledge among academics and teachers at career counselling sessions, seminars and discussions.

However, it must be said that the Army is hardly proactive in reducing these gaps. Even something as small as the Army calendar finds its way only to Army HQ and other offices whereas every single copy should be on the walls of schools, colleges, coffee houses, factories etc. It may seem to be an insignificant move but could go a long way in inducing people to take a keen interest in the affairs of the Army.

Making it a two way street the academics and teachers need to be addressed quickly and assisted in understanding what the Army is all about – the ultimate goal, after all is to impart information and share experiences.

Judiciary

Very often, the judiciary is required to make decisions on issues linked to the Army, especially in areas where insurgency is prevalent. It is unfair to expect advocates and judges to be able to imagine the reality, not having been exposed to it and yet, it has a job to do.

It will be mutually beneficial for both the Army and the legal system for the judiciary and connected people to actually know the Army.

Nothing can be more frustrating than to arrest a terrorist or insurgent with a weapon (firing at you), hand him over to the police only to find the individual out on bail shortly thereafter. To put it bluntly, if the Army's trust in the judicial system wavers, other problems will crop up soon enough. Therefore, a basic understanding of each other needs to be ensured.

In other areas it is to the credit of the judiciary that it is held in high esteem. There may be cause to take a second look at the methodology involved when the judiciary deals with cases pertaining to the Army. All services personnel, in fact, because most do not have the money to pay lawyers and, more important, cannot be present whenever needed. A general approach of dealing more quickly would benefit the armyman. Likewise, the armyman must learn to utilise the privileges fairly (most of them do) and not try and take the system for a ride.

Media

Arrogance in terms of the "we know it all" maxim is one aspect of the media that really irks Army personnel. This is a generalisation because there are some media personalities who do take care to present the right picture but their numbers, unfortunately, are not large. What are the weaknesses in general?

* Lack of knowledge about the Army as an organisation and its function.

* The lack of an eye for detail: even reputed TV programmes/newspapers etc constantly slip up. One TV programme (through a 15-minute coverage) continuously referred to 17 PARA FIELD REGIMENT as 17 PARA MILITARY REGIMENT (which implies that it does not belong to the Army at all). Glitches and gaffes, if they had to be listed, would become an interesting serial.

* Often the media wants to be "looked after" well.

* There are hardly any correspondents who have specialised in Army or defence studies.

* Egos are oversized because they know they can get away with virtually anything.

* Media takes sides - often of convenience.

* On TV networks interviewers lack knowledge, the choice of panels is not appropriate and the manner in which a discussion is conducted is far from satisfactory.

* The concept of war correspondents does not exist. Of course, there are pretenders who think being near a gun area is being in the war zone which, of course, is a fallacy.

The main cause of all this and more is lack of information, exposure and experience. Some of the fault lies with the media no doubt but a major share has to be borne by the Army. Where does the Army go wrong?

* Only eulogising media coverage is wanted - whereas objective coverage should be the focus.

* Use/post ineffective PR personnel (though some have been very good): they try to make up by "ensuring" that the senior officers' photographs appear in print or on screen.

* Acceptance of a purely civilian Defence PR which overrides Army PR.

(During an interview with the late Melville D'Mello the author was told, "One must be in love with the Army if one wants to do justice to any media coverage. It is not a job; it has to be a passion. If you have not experienced with the Army the uncanny silence between bursts of shelling and firing you have not even touched the tip of the iceberg. How I wish I was younger and with the troops".)

Note: In 1987-88 the author interviewed a lot of people for two dissertations. The interview with Late Mr. D'Mello is of September 1987.

The question, therefore, is how can a person from the Information Service coordinate defence PR. The earlier this arrangement is made to fly out of the window the better it will be.

* The Army's "face" in schools and colleges is prominent because of its very absence. It is simply beyond comprehension why decently produced posters, calendars, recruitment brochures, information brochures are not freely available in academic institutions. In fact, posters must be so

good that Army personnel in general and the PR organisation in particular ought to be flooded with requests for them.

* Not utilising in-house talent: There is no dearth of good writers, photographers, presenters in the Army but have absolutely no idea about how to utilise them. This once again reflects on the poor quality of macro planning - senior officers need to rectify this by educating themselves first. Even for an MOD Annual Report the MOD relies sometimes on civilian photographers (and ends up paying a hefty fee in cash or kind). The Annual Report is not a photography book! Since writing is not genuinely encouraged, the Army is not capable of putting out more presentable material that would be appreciated by a larger reading audience.

* Reactive PR: The Army is forever reacting to media stories. While this is necessary at times, it would reduce if the Army kept the public better informed by putting out information on their own. Reactions (rebuttals) invariably get lost in the newspaper pages whereas the first story stays in people's minds.

In this era of information overload one cannot do without the media. It would be better if the Army understood and utilised the media more effectively. It is heartening to note that the Army is developing a website - they need to nurture it and make responses real time.

General Public

While the Army may have to take a major share of the blame for not keeping people well informed, it must be taken note of that they are not the only ones to default. Parents, teachers, schools – all these are responsible for a balanced education. The lack of knowledge about a major instrument of government is unacceptable. The responsible ministries

(MOD, HRD etc) do not help in anyway. The awareness level must increase and everybody responsible should put his shoulder to the wheel.

Conclusion

Knowing one's Army (and the defence forces) has to feature as an educational cornerstone. The more one knows the more effective will be the analyses on expenditure and utilisation of the forces.

Any MOD Annual Report will provide an idea of focus and importance afforded to the Army or the forces. In one such recent report (of 111 pages), the Army occupied nine specific pages including four full-page photographs. The Army cannot afford to hide behind the MOD's apron strings – "inform all stake holders or be prepared to pay the price" is a lucid enough message.

9

The Facade of Caring

(Lip Service to Welfare)

A gradual decrease in the level of concern and commitment coupled with the lack of vision at senior levels has created huge gaps in "welfare" over the years. Though one has been witness to some action in certain areas in the past decade, it is lamentable that nothing really concrete has got done in the years gone by. Why did this happen? This query gives rise to even more questions:

* Were senior officers "too objective" and concentrated more on national needs than on the needs of their troops?

* Were senior officers unconcerned because they were not really affected? After all, they had/have their bungalows, plush offices, retinue of people to work for them – even their travels are normally on duty and so on.

* Did they lack the appropriate education to see things more clearly?

* Why did they show a singular lack of vision or concern?

* Were/are they so subservient to civilian authority?

* Were they more concerned about the cases in hand getting due approval?

* Did they (do they!) fail to put across a point of view comprehensively, convincingly and without any ambiguity? An old story that still does the rounds is regarding "separation allowance" - the government negotiator was told that he didn't have to seek approval for amounts upto Rs 600/- (at that point of time separation allowance was Rs 75/-). The Army top brass made a "brilliant" presentation and asked for Rs 150/- and the story ended right there.

* Is it that individual biases cloud analyses and tilt the very focus of most cases?

* Exposure to other avenues being extremely poor, senior officers bypass opportunities simply because they don't know what to push and they themselves remain insecure.

* Does emphasis on "self projection" deny senior officers the opportunity to evaluate other options? With all this underlying insecurity senior officers are wary of taking any advice lest it turns out to be a better solution and thereby their own clouded judgement becomes evident.

* Does hunger for power and authority and the capacity to display the same make rationale and common sense take one step back? One of the most apt examples of this is the annual mockery started in 1997 of the NCC games wherein apart from the DG (Director General) being photographed with VIPs "NOTHING" at all happens. If this is the primary focus of events such as these, how can one expect welfare to feature at all?

There is a need, therefore, for the Army to take a fresh look at the significance of the term "welfare". Perhaps a comprehensive study conducted by the College of Defence Management (or even three to four independent studies conducted by as many institutions) could come up with a few poignant points and suggest an agenda to work on. Once a long-term plan is evolved individual fancies and idiosyncrasies must not be allowed to interface with the focus.

Firstly, the Army needs to state clearly what welfare means - to each level and each group. Secondly, it must take into account needs as expressed by people and not as decided by the top brass. Thirdly, the Army needs to clearly spell out which activities can be carried out within the Army and which require outside intervention and help. Then, it must ensure that outside help is available. Fourthly, all aspects of welfare and their impact must be analysed, discussed and plans put in place. Fifthly, the Army must ensure welfare plans ultimately benefit **all** personnel. Sixthly, some semblance of permanence must be apparent in all projects and activities.

During the course of these "studies" a great many focus areas will emerge along with action plans. Quite understandably, it may not be possible for all the plans to be implemented immediately but this does not imply that lower priorities should be forgotten – though they may be delayed. Another important guideline to keep in mind before the commencement of this project is for senior officers to "listen" and "observe" rather than give their "views" (which in Army parlance means, "do it my way"). This attitude is a direct outcome of ideas of their so-called "good old days" (when they were inefficient, did not make necessary demands, accepted plans without properly analysing them etc). In fact, the management concept of SYM (Shut Your Mouth) can aptly be applied here.

To give a slight push start to such a venture some areas that need attention are listed below:-

* Look After Yourselves. Take the cue from politicians and bureaucrats who are experts at building nests and feathering them too. If the Army does not look after itself no one else will - this, at least, should be clear after over 50 years of chaotic mismanagement.

* Training Centres. Centres get so many young people ever so often but they are simply put to the grind. Centre Commandants, due to the lack of a genuine interest in welfare, cannot proudly state the following: "so many recruits who were eligible have been selected for NDA" or "so many have been spotted for further academic coaching and onward selection to become officers" or "so many have been spotted for a specific talent" or "so many are more suited for a different trade and have been sent" or "so many have been spotted for further review and selection for ACC (Army Cadet College)" and so on. Centre Commandants have a major role to play at the entry and exit levels as also in organising training/internships outside of the environment throughout the career of a soldier.

* Appraisal System. Must be utilised to look at and perpetuate development and achievement of potential of individuals - across the board. In addition to this, people in command must have this capacity for welfare mentioned in the ACR.

* Financial Advice. Money makes the world go round – competent, timely and comprehensive financial advice needs to be given to all and commanders at all levels must assist individuals by monitoring.

* Resettlement. This is the single biggest welfare measure and has already been discussed in detail in a previous chapter.

* Accommodation. As per the current rules of authorisation of government accommodation for families of other ranks, an Infantry soldier can hope to live with his family in such accommodation for a period of six months in a cycle of eight-nine years. RIDICULOUS you may say - but this is the situation at the grassroots level. And the Army has the audacity to claim it is looking after its men's welfare. A little explanation is perhaps in order. If the strength of an Infantry Battalion is 800 and authorised accommodation (which is mostly not available) is 14% the Battalion would have 112 quarters. If even 70% were family members then 560 people would want accommodation. In a three year cycle (if the unit spends three years in a peace station) at the most five periods of six months can be organised. So, an individual can hope to stay with his family for six months. Thus, it works out to field three years: peace three years: field three years. The reason to look at this sort of a cycle of nine years is because it gives a more realistic picture. In one year the unit may be out on exercises etc for over three months; it may not spend three years in a peace station and since during the separation period their children would have grown quite a bit, the peace - field six-year cycle becomes irrelevant. There is something called CILQ (Compensation in Lieu of Quarters) but the amount is so insignificant that one cannot hire accommodation with that money - but in this too there are ceilings. All in all, the situation is absurd. Thirty years ago, it did not pose a problem because very few wanted their families to accompany them on their postings – today, the reverse holds true. If the Army cannot find suitable and adequate accommodation for the wives and children why talk of welfare at all? The solutions lie in providing suitable accommodation according to individual choice anywhere in the country – so that one can consider making it one's own house at any point of time. At least, the families of the

armymen can get the right kind of education and exposure. The problem of both parents not being available for the children does have its own drawbacks but some neutralisation is provided for. Properly thought out and extended, it is possible for each armyman to contribute a little over a long period and possess a house of his own when he needs it (For God's sake keep the AWHO (the Army Welfare Housing Organisation) hoax out of this scheme)!

* Skill Training. The armyman gives all his time to the Army. There are no eight-hour shifts, trade unions etc, so he can easily be compensated for some of that time through training in some other skill other than the Army training. It may take the form of a hobby or an educational course (through distance education). Each individual, however, must be trained (in something officially recognisable) and allowed to practice a skill that he can put to use when no longer in uniform.

* Time Management: A number of precious hours come to naught in the time spent by the Army in waiting for VIPs, preparing for visits, inspections and the like. Coupled with this is the fact that there is absolutely no repair accountability – therefore the exercise becomes one in futility as programmes often get changed due to certain last moment glitches. The result? Colossal wastage that gets accentuated by people going overboard in ensuring what is known as the "Havildar Major Time". If an event is scheduled to take place at 8 AM the bulk of the people will be in position by 7 AM because every link in the chain of command demands a little safety margin. If this time is effectively utilised there will be ample time to actually work on welfare.

* Development Programmes. The Army needs to invest in various development programmes as per individual choice

and supported by a little counselling. Every individual should be put through such a programme at least once every 3-4 years.

* Common Causes. Given the present state of politics and bureaucracy in the country, lobbying has become a necessity. The time has come for people at large to support Army welfare activities as a common cause. Ultimately society will have nothing to lose; it may even gain from this.

* Travelling. Back in 1984, it was the suggestion of one unit that instead of relying on an Indian Air Force courier to ferry personnel from the East to Delhi, it would be more economical and definitely more comfortable to use civilian aircraft. However, wheels within wheels must have kept such a decision at bay. In 1998/99 such a service has commenced and in more directions than one. The Air Force charged the Army heavily and made the Army personnel feel quite unwanted (in their own courier) and they (Air Force) used the courier as their own fiefdom (what with absurdly early reporting times, poor food lousily packed that people paid for, lack of courtesy and so on). It is a good thing that sense has finally prevailed – this is another of those cases which is a clear indication of the lack of concern among senior officers/ decision makers. The Indian Army is quite pronouncedly north bound; therefore air couriers or special trains all head for Delhi. A detailed analysis will be required to make a decision on how the other zones are to be handled - some seats on selected flights or charter once a fortnight. Of railway movement the less said the better. The Army has neither made the demand for nor received an adequate number of seats/berths on all trains frequently used by Army personnel. Result: you find Army personnel in their uniforms making do with whatever space that is available. The lack of a fixed Army quota on trains and poor leave planning by units

are the crux of the problem. Of course, the railways are partly to blame - but the lion's share goes to the Army for its absence of foresight, poor planning and rank lack of concern. Processed correctly there is no reason for not having an adequate number of seats/berths being allocated to the Army on all trains; after all, if not utilised they are always available to the Railways. Typically, the Army in its wisdom pushed the wrong horse and got special trains to run for leave parties. If managed properly, this would not be a bad thing. But since these trains never run on time, the facilities are often out of order, leave parties coming from remote areas fail to reach on time, these "specials" are unsuccessful. Obviously the staff and decision-makers did not carry out an in-depth analysis of this. Some senior officer must have said "let's run a special train" and so it was planned. Military Specials (which convey units) are in such a pathetic condition (in terms of bogies, maintenance, timing halts etc) one would think these trains were being run as "charity".

* Living Conditions. Since Army troops do not happen to complain very frequently they are made to live in awful living conditions. Dark bunkers dripping bashas, tentage that is pathetically inadequate, bunkers with poor heating (in high altitudes). The list can go on. Observe two scenarios: **One**: a brigade is moved from its location to assist counter insurgency operations in another area: they are given no barracks, no requisitioned buildings, no bashas, no tents (the formation is not authorised tentage in its permanent locations) and the monsoons are already in full swing. Without toilets, two officers share a 40-pounder tent (a tall person's feet will stick out). Imagine the state of affairs! Yet, the formation is loaded with operational tasks. Except for the Indian Army, I do not believe any group would tolerate this kind of shoddy arrangement and still deliver the goods. **Two**:

a formation is moved from its peace station location to assist counter insurgency operations in the West - units arrive and find no accommodation. Here, luckily, the units have tentage but the monsoon season is at its peak. A veterinary hospital, which is not in use, is cleaned up to accommodate important equipment like ammunition. To make things a little comfortable unit commanders spend money from unit funds. On a request higher HQ allots money to the units for the "welfare" of troops. After seven months when the formation is returning to its location the units are asked to leave behind the "welfare" stores. Really annoyed with this puerile behaviour, units and formation HQ send cheques of the same amount to the higher HQ. So much for welfare! The money was meant ostensibly for troops that had been inducted from peace stations, leaving families behind.

* Looking After Families. If families are well looked after the armyman can overlook a number of the problems he faces. Therefore, activities which can enable the families of Army personnel to benefit, perhaps the capacity to stand on their own feet economically and so on must be pursued. In case an Army personnel dies in counter insurgency operations or in Siachen or because of an accident while on duty, in all fairness the wife must draw the same pay till superannuation (in the normal course). This would be welfare in the actual sense of the term.

* Education. Providing facilities and support for better education for children, even the wives and Army personnel themselves would perhaps be the best welfare. Improving one's all round status must surely rate high on any individual's priority list. The Army has made some commendable efforts but it still has a long way to go. There are a large number of Army schools and a few Army Public Schools which eases the problems of admissions for the

children. Yet, in every station the "feeling of being welcome" is missing. In the Army Public School, Delhi, for example, there seems to be no urgency to admit children coming from other places. The school seems more keen on adhering to rules - scheduled dates for entrance examinations, retests in case a child hasn't done too well (of course this happens because the school loses half the papers most of the time). Perhaps a couple of more retests - in the meantime the child is missing classes. Absurd but true, and such a situation comes to pass because the members of the governing body do not take the trouble to learn about education. Leading from such a base you have a perfect example of a school not being run properly, of corruption and so on. Getting the "right" people together to run these schools is important - people can't be just detailed for such jobs as the Army does. The answer lies in finding the right talent (from within the Army or from ex-servicemen or, if neither works, from outside) on contract basis. This would probably ensure the people make a good job of it. The Army must supervise and intervene when the situation so requires. Don't have a civilian principal taking everybody for a ride. It takes ages for the Army top brass to react and by then irreparable damage has already been done. A great deal of vision is required to build up a proper schooling system and the Army owes it to its personnel and their children. Since admission into professional colleges is difficult the Army has done well to open a few institutions though some are located in the most unlikely of places, the Management Faculty in Jabalpur with College of Materials Management for one. Though why, when there are no other Management training facilities around, no major industries yet, the Army chose to do so is beyond comprehension. Secunderabad, Mumbai, Pune, Delhi, Calcutta, Bangalore were viable options but Jabalpur it had to be! It can only be hoped such absurdities do not recur. A study to consider future needs (long term plan) ought to be carried out and plans made accordingly. The contact level and intensity needs to be expanded to include children, wives and personnel. All training/education need not be in-house; the Army must seek effective collaboration with universities, business schools, reputed teaching institutions both in India and abroad. Teachers taking the organisation for a side (as in Army Public School, Delhi) must not be allowed. Contracts must be carefully drairn up and teachers should be thrown out if students interests are not foremost on their minds.

* Uniform Scale of Pay. Moving toward the upper level all JCOs and other ranks should have a uniform pay scale. Currently, the Infantryman is at the bottom of the compensation list even though he faces the maximum hardship, deprivation and risk to life.

* Uphold Prestige. Downgrading of levels just to "get the job done" is incorrect. Everyone up the chain needs to be consciously involved in ensuring this. Making NCOs cut grass (an example previously quoted of what is actually happening in the NCC) or sending senior officers to follow up on files with fairly junior people in the MOD, forcing people to travel without reservations (due to sudden decisions) - all these lead to a lowering in the status of an armyman and should not be allowed. This needs to be extended to ceremonials like Beating Retreat, the Republic Day Parade etc. In fact, Army officers (as also other service personnel) should refrain from attending these functions. Why? Because all the arrangements are seen to by the Army yet the invitation cards remain in the hands of some civilian in the MOD who decides when Colonels should attend and when Major Generals should (and where they should sit)! This is disgusting but accepted by the

Army without a murmur of protest. Discontent regarding this matter is extremely intense and it is a wonder that some semblance of dignity has not sought to be retained by returning the invitation cards.

* Information. A lot of fruitful and beneficial activities that could be undertaken by Army personnel and families (during and after the service period) are left undone because of a lack of information. The list could be very long but it is time the Army woke up to these realities and benefited from them. Some points are given here:-

* Solar Energy. Use of solar energy is nowhere near as popular as it should be. Loans, interest rates, subsidies given etc must be made known to people and they should be encouraged to utilise them. But a fair guess would be that the AG (Adjutant General) or QMG (QuarterMaster General) themselves have no idea about these details so who will they guide anyway?

* NCC. For the children the NCC is a wonderful opportunity to gain more exposure apart from the school curriculum. But most of the Army Schools and Kendriya Vidyalayas do not have NCC because they wonder as to who will fund half. The Centre and states share the expenditure and Army Schools/KVs don't belong to the state. The AG must resolve this instead of just writing letters which have no meaning and not yielded any results so far.

* Train Commanders. A lot of general welfare is linked to getting things done by other organisations. Most commanders fail miserably in this regard and to cover up their shortcomings, pretend to be far too busy with operational tasks, formation routine etc. In effect, commanders at all levels either do not know or do not care

to know about these aspects and the troops suffer. The Army has no system whatsoever of preparing commanders to deal with these aspects; they are expected to simply make do. Those commanders who take the trouble to educate themselves can ensure a far better deal for the troops. Some of the areas that all commanders need to be trained in are given below (some may not be easily applicable to certain locations but knowledge will be useful because some divisional commanders who have commanded brigades in remote field areas are likely to try and bulldoze their way and push organisations into bigger trouble say in dealing with Contonment Boards):

MES. Commanders must understand the nuances of MES working. The ingenious methods they have of taking people for a ride would require a separate book. Suffice to know that rules and regulations exist and if followed in toto will benefit the Army. Contracts must be read in detail. As a catalyst to learning here are a few points:

(i) Pathways. Repairing and cementing of pathways/stairs is a favourite of the MES because it costs a lot, disappears in the monsoons and snow and the whole process can be repeated!

(ii) Construction. The MES rates are always high and include departmental charges.

Cantonment Boards. A well-established system if properly utilised can benefit troops living there. Requires a great deal of reading and understanding.

Station Headquarters. This HQ looks after basic administration and therefore a clear understanding of its functioning is essential for commanders.

10

Missing the Beat Once Too Often

(Media and the Army)

Being a war correspondent once held a charm of its own – there was an aura of romance, danger and adventure that surrounded the job. They were actually considered a breed apart. That was the time when the media took the Army seriously - because they knew the Army and vice versa. This mutual respect still prevails in some western countries where correspondents risk their lives to be able to report accurately, be it from Bosnia, Yugoslavia, Angola or East Timor or anywhere else where the action is taking place.

In the Indian context, however, the scenario has been almost consistently dismal. Neither do media personae wish to learn nor do they want to experience the hardships that are part and parcel of such a job. True, there are some rare exceptions, but they are few and far between. Among the older lot, the late Melville De Mello, Situ Mullick and Victor Longer come to mind. After that there has been a general blank. In 1962, except for Victor Longer no Indian correspondent stayed on, even in Tezpur. In 1971, in the Chittagong sector, we saw the first Indian "war" correspondent three days after the surrender. But the media holds the upper hand in the Indian context for three reasons:

one, the Army is quite ignorant about the media; two, senior officers only look at the media in the context of good public relations; and three, the media is not accountable for anything. Location studies, like the one conducted by the Press Council in 1991 on the Kunan-Poshpura (J&K), are rare. Even more rarely does the media come up with truly objective reporting. One has to realise that the media plays an extremely important role where the Army is concerned, especially in a democracy (even in the almost free-for-all situation like ours). After all, the country must know what their Army is up to since a large portion of the tax payers' money goes into keeping the Army in being.

Thanks to some of the private TV channels, the Kargil conflict could be analysed at close quarters, albeit on the screen. Audiences could actually follow what was going on at the front. Even though the clips were all from the gun areas, the footage was certainly better than the usual file photos which is what Doordarshan would have probably churned out.

If all were not as it should be, a brief analysis would not be out of place.

General

In general the media is found wanting in certain specific areas.

Lack of Knowledge: The urge to make do with the barest minimum of knowledge is the first major drawback of the media. One may conveniently say that enough information is not forthcoming from the Army but that does not provide the media with a licence to show or write anything. The onus of gaining knowledge lies with the media. It is time people stopped making excuses and constantly passing the buck –

blaming the Army for everything that goes wrong (the reverse is also true - more on that later in this chapter).

Reading: Media personae either do not read or do not read enough or do not read the right material. There can be very little argument on this count. Most correspondents suffer from inadequate background knowledge.

Accuracy: Inaccuracies inevitably creep into stories and presentations and there seems to be no concern to ensure the accuracy of reports. Even the terminology used is often filled with errors.

Lack of Detail: Often, vital details are missed out and the Army cannot help but feel (perhaps rightly) that they have been left out on purpose. This seeps into the areas of providing partial truth for a whole story.

Accountability: Accountability and responsibility seem to be alien to the media at times. Since the Army rarely responds, the media has a field day and gets away with saying and showing anything. This is quite apparent from the headings often seen in newspapers.

Opinions and Biases: Here it is not only the biases of media people that come through but also the straight reporting of other peoples' opinions. Take the example of insurgency: it erupts due to "pathetic" (poor would be too mild a word) administration. We basically mean the bureaucracy here. Certain retired bureaucrats, having mucked up the situation thoroughly, actually have the gall to state that the Army is interested in prolonging insurgency. This is nothing short of utter nonsense. They further have the audacity to question what the Army has done in all these years. This is borne out of sheer ignorance but the media reports such statements ad lib without bothering to either analyse or provide proper comment. Similarly, there are correspondents who hold the view that armymen are "paid to die". When they are confronted with an analysis they simply turn a deaf ear. Loyalty to the country (according to them) is the responsibility of defence personnel alone. In short, most media persons are far too opinionated and have little or no depth.

Acknowledgements: Very rarely are due acknowledgements stated by the media, except in some films and TV programmes. It is tantamount to taking full credit for half the work.

Presenting the Uniformed Person: Aside from a few exceptions, the visual media presents the armyman totally inaccurately. The total lack of care is astounding. Inevitably, some vague ideas of the director are reflected in any programme. Since it takes very little to get the essential details right, one tends to feel that the mockery is on purpose. There are some films however which have taken great care to get the details right. But the majority of them show armymen with unkempt and long hair, the shirt buttons open, wrong lanyards, an ASC badge displayed (is it more easily available? or more noticeable?) for fighting arms - the list of visual goof ups is never ending.

Roles That Should Be Played

In a large democracy like ours, the media needs to play a few roles quite seriously. One may even say it is honour bound to do so. Some of the important roles are given below.

Information Provider: The general public gets most of its information regarding the forces from the media, therefore there is the responsibility aspect. In a study carried out a few years ago, the major sources of information (more than one source was indicated) were newspapers, TV, people known, radio and magazines.

Debater: The media must create a platform for debate on issues that have a large impact. Issues like the defence/Army budget, human rights, deployment of the Army on tasks other than the primary ones; resettlement and others could be discussed to increase general awareness.

Analyser: Analyse the needs of the Army and the roles it plays. This would provide in-depth information about its functioning.

Image Projector: To project an accurate image, the Army should not expect the media to carry out a public relations exercise on its behalf. In this, the film world has a major role to play and must seek professional assistance from Army HQ. If the media takes this role seriously they will always check details before putting out a story. Sensationalism has to be played down because in any case the Army does not fight back.

Mature Mediator. Perhaps the most difficult role to play (and rarely played) but an essential role nevertheless. The media would do well to assuage the sentiments of both sides (whenever there is a conflict) rather than taking sides. Difficult but necessary, and for this role media personae have to become more mature.

Roundup

It is very clear that the media has a major role to play in a democratic country's Army. If this role has to be played well, media persons must climb off their high horses and discard their "know it all" attitude. They have to make an effort to become more knowledgeable. They ought to welcome opportunities to talk and discuss and stop carrying around thin sensitive skins which get irritated if they are not "looked after" well. They should remember that they are out on an assignment and not on some pleasure jaunt.

Army's Commitment

Having said so much about the media one needs to take the Army to task for pathetically failing in the business of providing the media with accurate information and taking them into confidence. PR is a specialised subject after all but the Army continues to "make do" with whoever is available. The PR organisation needs an overhaul. Some of the areas that require attention are:

People: Find suitable people (with a flair for PR), train them well and locate them appropriately for the best impact.

Wherewithal: Wherewithal to carry out various duties like informing, correcting, writing etc must be made available in terms of telephones, transportation, data base and so on.

Course: The course that is the orientation programme for journalists and media persons must be sensibly organised. The schedule must take into account the media's convenience and be held at media centres. The Intelligence School (of the Army) has no business conducting this course in any case. Periodicity must be such that anyone who is interested can attend the course.

Information Material: These must be produced in adequate numbers and distributed. A special handout for media personnel covering most of the general queries is a must. A few years ago when there were 46,000 higher secondary schools, 5,000 degree colleges and 160 engineering colleges - the Recruitment Directorate had "ordered" for only 13,000 copies of booklets indicating eligibility conditions etc. How many booklets reached the right people is a matter of conjecture. Therefore, what is (should be !!!) needed for media personnel is not even known.

Proactive: The Army must at all times be willing to go to the media with information and be prepared to present the comprehensive picture (as the media person is often genuinely short of time).

Legal Action: It is a must to initiate legal action against any media house that reports a falsity. This needs to be done as quickly as possible. At least a certain measure of accountability will thus be ensured.

Build Bridges: With the media so that understanding is good and time is not wasted in post-facto explanations.

Army is not insulated: This needs to be understood by and explained to all ranks.

Conclusion

The various genres of the media must be utilised for an overall plan to inform and instruct. Understanding the media is the armyman's responsibility and reporting objectively is the media's. Getting to an underground insurgent leader and publishing his story without comments from the Army is unethical and only reeks of sensationalism.

The arrogance of the media needs to be tempered. The Army must not have the "stop – go" policy – one day the orders clearly state that "you can speak" – the next it will be changed to "no one is to speak". This creates utter confusion. The Army must provide effective information at all times and be prepared to answer questions.

The media, on their part, must develop the courage of conviction (honesty really) to say "I don't know or don't understand - please explain this to me". The Army's commitment to provide useful and necessary information must not be diluted.

The media owes it to the nation to present an objective picture about the Army (and the other services as well) and they will really have to work hard at it.

Personal Note

Some years back the author had, in a dissertation (on Army Public Relations) made some copy suggestions for advertisements. The dissertation copy was with the Deputy Chief of the Army Staff (DCOAS), Directorate General of Military Intelligence etc. No acknowledgements were made, but the striking similarities with the current advertisements do raise eyebrows!

"Are you man enough for a manly career?"

"The Army lives life to the full"

"The Army runs on Izzat"

"Nam, Namak, Nishan – that's the Army"

"Dust storms to the snows"

"High technology and adventure go hand in hand in the Army"

"Fully integrated Indian"

"Dynamics, that's the word" .

11

Fauji Ko Gussa Kyon Aata Hai

(Why a soldier gets angry)

Army personnel seem to be, by and large, content among themselves and avoid outside contact as far as possible. A bit of an anachronism because the armyman hails from the same social system. The reason perhaps lies in the fact that he finds what goes on outside rather annoying and therefore tends to stay within the olive green cycle. The Army belongs to the nation at large and the nation needs to take a closer look at the aspects that annoy the armyman, both within the Army and outside it and rectify whatever is possible for the good of the Army in particular and the country in general.

Irritants are many and this is bound to be what with such a large Army and such wide variety existing in the country. The attempt here will be to provide a direction to the search. But it won't have all the answers though.

External Environment

Lack of Support: A general feeling that the Army is taken for granted and support is lacking is evident from the environment. It is not as if the armyman is looking for favours. What then is he looking for? Perhaps, a little consideration and some understanding.

Lack of Exchange Value. Society (thanks to politicians, rules and regulations, power and authority etc) has become fairly corrupt (very corrupt if one is to endorse international studies). In such an environment, the armyman is constantly made to feel the lack of exchange power - he has nothing to get in return (licence, police protection, a good word, money) except perhaps buy a few things from the CSD canteen at a subsidised rate.

Follow Instructions. The Army religiously follows all instructions whereas everyone else freely flouts them. The Cabinet says "........increase retirement age......" and it is implemented irrespective of the turmoil caused; when parliament is in session "...... don't leave your offices till the session winds up......" and officers stay back doing nothing. Why? Because someone passed on instructions.

Comparison. In an open society comparisons cannot be avoided. While one does not compare often with the corporate world, the armyman does see the well looked after bank official going on strikes, he experiences delays while going home because of numerous illegal bandhs delaying trains, he sees little work getting done in government offices and so on. When he compares himself with non-Army persons, the armyman cannot help the irritation that creeps in.

Visits/Inspections. Every now and then people (in groups, as individuals, as committees) come on visits and even though the armyman puts up a brave and smiling front he knows nothing ever gets done for his good by any of these visits. Of course, he also realises that most of these visits are, in fact, thinly camouflaged holidays. He hates them!

Protocol. Protocol and precedence in rank has been systematically turned on their heads and the armyman is aware that the system is working against him because given a level playing field the others (who have for no reason, been raised in status) will prosper while he will never get anywhere. This needs to be restored rationally and soon. Calamities do not come with too much of a notice - all concerned should consider themselves warned.

Queues and Bribes. Since the armyman is mostly short of time (short leaves, no extensions at will etc) he hates the delays that are thrust upon him. While he doesn't mind a reasonable and disciplined queue, he deplores the way other people bribe their way to the front of the queue or the fact that he ends up wasting his time and not getting the job done. Not that the armyman has not learned to give bribes (the environment was not created by him), he still does not like it.

Hidden Agendas. Brought up on a diet of openness, the Armyman hates hidden agendas. For example, a RM's attempts to dispose off Army land under some pretext or the other did not go down well with people.

Trips Abroad. Besides the exposure and experience they afford, trips abroad are always attractive. Bureaucrats always find themselves detailed on courses or missions or study teams which involve going abroad. Sabbaticals abroad are also common for bureaucrats. "Work harder and get less in return" seems to be the armyman's lot in life and most of them must be thoroughly cheesed off with it.

Lateral Mobility. A generalist's job can be done by anybody. Therefore the armyman cannot comprehend why he cannot get a tenure or two in other areas or departments which could ultimately increase his chances for a second career.

Apathy. Sometimes the very apathy of government organisations irks the armyman. To quote a personal example: In August 1998, my wife and I applied for passports. The police verification was done quickly enough but because we had truthfully given our previous address (we had arrived in Delhi in August 1997) as CIJWs (Counter Insurgency and Jungle Warfare School) located in Mizoram, we had to fill yet another set of forms with photographs. While forwarding the forms, I had indicated that my 32 years of commissioned service should be taken into account and the fact that in the Army we are frequently posted at different locations is also well known. But the Regional Passport Officer till date has not bothered to reply and the passports were ultimately issued (though no communication was issued to me) after the office of the External Affairs Minister raised a query. There is a myriad of such examples of the complete indifference that government organisations feel. In this aspect some corporate houses too tend to default but the majority of corporate houses respond quite well to inquiries placed by the Army.

Railways & Others. Most people think they have done the Army a big favour by providing special trains and allocating some seats on selected trains. A number of trains (especially the prestigious ones) have no quotas and special trains are in a pathetic condition. The same goes for other people to whom the armyman has to turn to get some jobs done - cement release, land registration etc.

Rules and Regulations. Rules and regulations have been made as if not to allow effective functioning is their main focus and providing business to certain individuals and organisations is the secondary aim. This results in frustration and finally people resort to lies or find roundabout (illegal) ways to function effectively. Rules and regulations must be thrown overboard en masse and a new set (practical, useful with adequate, not stranglehold, checks) put in place. To avoid being charged with over generalising let us look at a few areas.

* **Buying Stationery.** Stationary depots have long been redundant because they supply virtually nothing but without a NA (Not Available) certificate from them stationery can't be bought. Stationery has to be bought with three quotations and the payment is made by Regional CDAs (Controller of Defence Accounts) directly to dealers. Result - one, a fair amount of delay occurs and two, pleasing the people at the CDA office has to be looked into by the dealer otherwise the bills can be delayed eternally. Because of this only a few dealers are willing to go through this rigmarole and they extract their pound of flesh by charging a higher amount and also supply substandard items. What does an effective commander or staff officer do if he does not want to carry on like this? Instead of waiting he spends regimental funds (which are not meant for official work) or the more sensible (who don't mind sticking their necks out for the organisation) he pays the stationary dealer 10-15% and takes the amount in cash and buys directly from the wholesalers. As a result, the unit or HQ gets about double the stationery and far better quality. If this is the ground reality one can safely assume two things: first, the rules and regulations are stupid; two, some people are making money out of nothing (stationery dealers with links and personnel who pass the bills in the Regional CDAs).

* **Rations.** Apparently, all rules are in place regarding tenders, quality of supplies and so on. In order to obtain the contract quotes are so low that one can safely assume the contractor will supply less or supply different items or not supply at all. There are so called checks and purchase against contractor's risk is possible but not always feasible. This is because one, there may not be a major market available; two, by the time the contractor indicates "no supply" wholesalers may be closed and it is impractical to go to 30-40 retailers to buy the items; three, the item may not be available at all. Some of the main problem areas (the Army hierarchy is fully aware of these but is both lethargic and inefficient in resolving them) are:

* **Meat**. The contract rate is so low that the supplier always tries to supply items that are cheaper - eggs, chicken (in some places). Some tenders need to be rejected; the answer may lie in cooperatives supervised by the Army and run by ex-servicemen.

* **Fresh.** In Army parlance, it stands for vegetables and fruits. The outward picture is very colourful - vegetables are supplied as a very good mix (percentages are laid down), quality is fixed, sizes are fixed etc but below the true picture is rotten because the supplier will supply the cheapest vegetables and fruits and try and make up percentages later. Rules permit rejection of the supply but then what does the commander feed his troops? He curses the "rule" position and makes the best arrangements he can.

* **Coal.** Where coal is authorised for warming purposes the rule says the coal having been picked up from railway sidings is dumped at the supply depot. Units then have to collect it from the depot. The number of handlings naturally increase coal dust - a percentage is laid down but the unit is

left with the Hobson's choice of accepting excess coal dust and keeping people warm or fight the system and be left out in the cold. Some thinking local commanders get in touch with the supply authorities, send their own boys to the sites and bring loaded transport directly to the units thereby reducing extra handling, using less vehicles for collection and thereby trying to ensure good quality coal. Despite all this units are stuck with left over coal dust which they make into fuel balls - but that is not their job. Extensive use of solar and other non-conventional energy is needed but "rules" will not allow such investment.

Wearing of Uniform. There is an absolute lack of effective checks to ensure other people do not wear clothes/ uniforms which look similar to those worn by the Army. Yet security guards, office personnel, drivers etc wear uniforms similar to those worn by the Army and there is no move to stop them. In fact, accoutrements as worn by the Army (or the other services) cannot be worn by others (including police forces). The mockery continues in an even more perverted form in films. This total lack of respect for the uniform is irksome to say the least.

Use of Car Flags. Only the armed forces, according to existing rules, are allowed to fly flags on their vehicles. The others permitted to fly flags are, in addition to the Supreme Commander, ministers and diplomats. The average Indian (especially urbanite) is glued to cable TV but he refuses to absorb that even the highest ranking police officers in other countries do not fly car flags. Nowhere else in the world will you find a politician flying an outsize party flag and driving into the President's domain (Rashtrapati Bhawan). Since nobody cares, in India, virtually anyone and everyone can fly a flag. Tradition gives this prerogative to the armed forces and a very few exceptions as mentioned.

Use of Star Plates. Nowhere else in the world are star plates displayed on vehicles other than by the armed forces. But just take a look around – all and sundry, if they happen to be in a uniform of some kind, display star plates in India. Those who can't display them put up big designation (Chief Engineer etc) signs. While this last is useful for certain appointments like the Commissioner or Collector, it is unnecessary to display these designation signs when the car is unoccupied. Yet typically, it is conveniently left uncovered even when the vehicle is unoccupied.

School Admissions. The frequent moves and postings that being in the forces, especially the Army, entails, causes a lot of hassles. School admissions being such a long drawn out procedure, these moves unsettle not only the children of Army personnel but the parents as well. Instead of co-operating, school principals cause a lot of unnecessary fuss. There are certain government instructions but no one really pays heed to these. A few visits and a lot of requests, however, may produce results. Even in Kendriya Vidyalayas (which came into being to facilitate people in the government who are frequently transferred) the problem is enormous because the principals prefer false certificates (indicating seven postings) to admit children. The basic requirement of a good education is something everyone wishes for his or her children - even this, thanks to endless red tapism, is frequently denied.

Cleaning Up. Perhaps the single most annoying aspect of the external environment is that the Army is always involved in cleaning up the mess created by the "politician–bureaucrat" nexus. The mess that is caused by poor planning, lack of implementation, sheer neglect and often because of underhand contacts with criminals or corrupt businessmen. It could be a fire at a hill station, floods, drought, earthquake or railway accidents. Worse than even cleaning up is the lack of recognition from the politician or bureaucrat as they are busy looking for other returns. But, fortunately, people affected are genuinely grateful.

Bureaucracy. Perhaps the one single community that annoys the armyman uniformly is the bureaucracy. They delay cases, often sabotage them, insist on showing authority and have discovered innumerable spokes they can put in the wheels of functioning. One hears from reliable sources that because the bureaucracy did not want to pass out the total package given by the United Nations they continued to dilly dally while our contingent in Cambodia was reduced to actually having to beg for small necessities like toothpaste. There were serious disciplinary problems yet for all these the Commanders gallantly took the blame on the spot. The source of the problem - the bureaucrats, however chose to feign innocence. Perhaps even got a promotion for their "efforts". Except for the authority that is vested in them due to age-old rules, very few bureaucrats actually have anything going for them. If it weren't for getting approvals for cases and projects (thanks to the Indian system of authority devolving on the generally ignorant) there would be no reason to relate with them at all. This is certainly not to say that all bureaucrats are bad but the system certainly is rotten to the core.

Internal Environment

Putting the spotlight on the external environment is a good thing but one must accept there are a lot of things that annoy the armyman within the Army as well. Ostrichlike the Army carries on, pretending "all is well". There is a silver lining in that every now and then one does come across commanders who are genuine leaders and are prepared to look deep to try and combine happiness and effectiveness. One can only hope their tribe grows. But the fact is that there are too many commanders who do not really give a damn so long as their advancement is taken care of. Everyone agrees that a lot of changes for the better could be effected but nothing much gets done. In this, the senior officers are mainly responsible. For one, they perpetrate this status and two, allow continuation of the state. Troops and junior officers give a hundred percent of their loyalty and commitment and therefore, definitely deserve better.

Some senior officers make things worse by their multiple standards. They talk high morality and in the next breath throw all values to the winds when a politician promises to look into his case so that he can get an extension (against all rules and regulations) and get a promotion as well. The situation (in these cases) is pathetic. Worse, these same gentlemen want (order) their juniors to respect and obey them. They have to be grateful for basic Army discipline otherwise these senior officers would be booed every time they opened their mouths. If the base on which they stand has been stabilised - it would be on sycophancy - one can imagine the calibre of officers, JCOs and other ranks who will be well liked and allowed to get promotions. A dangerous trend which needs to be looked into. But then again the Indian Army is lucky because there are quite a few senior officers who don't fall into this cadre.

Some areas that definitely need introspection by the Indian Army are:

* **Reliance on Personality.** "Every commander has his own style" is a maxim that is carried too far and has come to signify merely giving in to the whims and fancies of

individuals. Even in training establishments there is a lack of continuity because everyone is trying to put his "stamp" on it. They are always in a hurry to prove the previous incumbent a fool. The maturity level is as low as it can get. The moment commanders change at any level an enormous amount of time is wasted in gauging preferences. At one point of time the College of Combat changed its emphasis of study of the 1971 war because the then Chief had commanded a particular corps during 1971. What one wishes to emphasise is that certain individual preferences sometimes have to be taken into account but making too many changes (just for the sake of change) is not acceptable.

* **Time Wastage.** Punctuality is a great asset of the Army but this virtue has its own drawbacks because of the excessive concern of senior officers. While punctuality is very much prevalent, time boundaries are frequently violated. The arrival time is fixed but departures are flexible, so one ends up not reaching some other place in time. Ultimately, it amounts to sheer lack of respect for other people's time. When I was commanding a Brigade, we were 4 1/2 hours driving time away from the Divisional HQ, and I was suddenly asked (ordered) to attend a dining out of a visiting senior officer. This happened to coincide with the dining out of one of the COs of the Brigade but reasoning had no place in that Division during that particular GOC's tenure. I attended that dinner and drove back at night - 12 hours spent for a stupid instruction the GOC did not want to change. Is it any wonder then that people sometimes ask (albeit under their breath) "who made this idiot a senior officer"? Personally, I have never excused that senior officer for wasting my time and not allowing me to 'dine out' a commanding officer of my own Brigade. These are individual instances - unfortunately they are almost the norm in the

Army. Protocol is always cited as the reason why. Since very little respect exists for other people's time (and seniors are rarely objective), a great deal of time gets wasted in waiting - waiting for the helicopters, for the motorcade, for the VIP to go, for the decision etc. Norms have been set for proper reception of the awaited guest (even if one has to travel a long way to "wait" at the airfield, helipad and so on). But if one is practical and stays in his work area all hell will break loose. Inspections and visits annoyingly start on the first day of the week, this ensures that the unit or HQ being visited wastes the entire Sunday in preparations. There are two other methods commonly used by senior officers to waste time: one: changes - change schedules, postpone them, ask for a programme or change them altogether and two: cancel visits at the last moment. Given its unblemished reputation of punctuality, the Army needs to seriously look inwards and cut out time wasters. Lest one forgets, there is a unique ploy used by senior officers (those who abhor actually working) to ask for a presentation after a detailed case is put up to him in writing. These are just some of the endless methods utilised by certain people to waste time - no wonder they are so "busy being busy".

* **Lack of Concern.** Very often one comes across officers unit commanders upward) who manifest a total "lack of concern". It is so critical for these people to look and be "important" that they misuse the basic disciplinary sense in the Army and roughride over everyone thereby spreading discontentment all around. Such people must be spotted early and run aground because these are basically weak and insecure officers. On 15th August and 26th January, traditionally, officers go to the JCOs Mess and JCOs go to the Officers' Mess respectively (depending on what has been in vogue in that unit). (Without mentioning any names) A GOC visiting a Brigade is

scheduled to leave after his visit in the morning on the 25th of January. Suddenly, he decides to stay on till the 26th and to make a mark of his importance he chalks out a different programme altogether. On the 26th he decides to make two unscheduled visits along the way (still in the Brigade area): Result: troops and officers are busy on Republic Day and the Brigade Commander is very late to welcome the JCOs into the Mess. To the armyman this incident may seem far-fetched yet it is true and is hardly an exception. It was so important for the general to show his dominance that "lack of concern" and his own insecurity manifested quite clearly. He could just as well have rested, taken a trip through the forests (the location was a hill station with lovely Deodar forests; and the general's wife was accompanying him) on the 25th and left early on the 26th. But no. The Army needs to look into this failing very seriously – leave aside all the other ills, it also promotes sycophancy because subordinate commanders are expected to say (unthinkingly) "No problem, Sir".

* **Inability to Handle Dissent.** Brought up on a "Yes Sir" routine, the Army has ensured that it is incapable of handling dissent. This shows up repeatedly in the arbitrary way cases, suggestions are disposed with keeping in view the top man's preference. A direct spin off is a culture of "Don't disagree", "Don't stick your neck out" and, therefore, a state of inertia or status quo sets in because you cannot even walk (forget progress) without friction. Dissent needs to be analysed and dealt with in a mature fashion if benefits are to be drawn. Of course, some commanders go one up - in a conference they will ask for suggestions - not listen to any - give a decision and then proclaim it is "our" decision so there should be no cribs outside this room. Perhaps the single greatest reason for the Army's lack of genuine progress is this failing. Given all the advantages of structure, teams, chain of

command, close relations, professionally well qualified people and so on, it is really unfathomable why the Army cannot handle dissent in a mature fashion. The damage done is irredeemable: because ideas are not floated around, people stop reading, and the safe path is the well beaten one and the safe methodology is "don't do anything extra" - successfully killing the energetic spirit in all ranks. When one looks around, one sees a lot of senior officers (God forbid, some may even hold the top post) who are senior today simply because they didn't ruffle any feathers along the way and did "nothing wrong" (which does not mean that they did "a lot of right"). How can we expect such people to take a stand, make effective decisions or benefit from ideas because of dissent? The picture is gloomy, if not alarming, and the Army needs to rectify this state of affairs quickly but surely (with some permanence). Feedback (objective), which is now prominent by its absence, needs a fresh impetus.

* **Resource Wastage.** Compromising on quality is not advisable but the unnecessary wastage of resources and material needs careful consideration. Take the example of "cleanliness" - every time a VIP visits a place "chuna–geru" (whitewashing and painting) is done all over again- or a VIP's wife likes the colour pink so the guest room gets done up in pink. This is frivolous wastage at the rudimentary level. Taken to ordnance depots, embarkation headquarters (where imported items arrive), transit facilities and so on, resource wastage is colossal. Unfortunately, a lot of these are linked to rules and regulations, therefore, maintaining status quo is a comfortable way out. The Army cannot afford to be lethargic in these respects. If the authority to expend money is judiciously decentralised resources would also be better utilised and we would not hold such massive inventories. Without appointing committees (which the Army is perpetually doing) and wasting

time, there is a need to put together younger creative teams to find solutions. Older and senior officers "often" (not always) have experience but most are blinkered in their thinking, therefore, unsuitable to look for innovative solutions. Resource redeployment, utilisation and, if need be, disinvestment are critical to the Army's well being.

* **Lack of Growth.** Genuine growth is not effectively planned for in the Army. In some ways it is convenient for senior officers because it is easier to handle officers without an all round growth (officers with an education can ask questions). But the problem goes deeper than this: officers without an all round education cannot do their jobs well when they become senior. This is the main reason why one encounters, ever so frequently, senior officers who are overly concerned about siting of automatics or platoons or companies. But they know nothing else despite excellent libraries, courses and optimal exposure. To them, it is more important to have the helmets (whether they are needed or not) fitted right rather than the heads. This may seem like an unduly harsh assessment but it is better, in this instance, to err on the plus side. Exceptions to the rule are what keep the system going. However, a large number of senior officers have not even bothered to educate themselves adequately. Even though a lot of them go through excellent courses like the Higher Command Course, Long Defence Management Course, National Defence College, they reap no benefits which can be of use to the Army simply because they are so busy being important. If senior officers are not secure, well informed and well read they cannot think freely which in turn will not allow them to create an environment of growth. It is so important for them to "succeed" that "growth" ends up flying out of the window. It is this environment which leads to lack of delegation and over centralisation. Commanders, at all levels, are not being allowed to grow. "Success" being critical – going overboard to ensure this

starts off and where a Lance Naik (one striper) would do, a senior major would be detailed - or a general would tell a Colonel or a Brigadier to "personally take the file to the Under Secretary and get it cleared". On the surface, all seems well (and people complain about the "youngsters") but that's a facade - the problem lies with senior officers (in this I would take Lt. Col. upwards) in an upward skew.

* **Decision-Making.** Everyone is (or should be) aware of the decision making process but make too many decisions sans analyses. To analyse the problem areas of decision making in the Army, a recap of the decision making chain is called for. It follows:

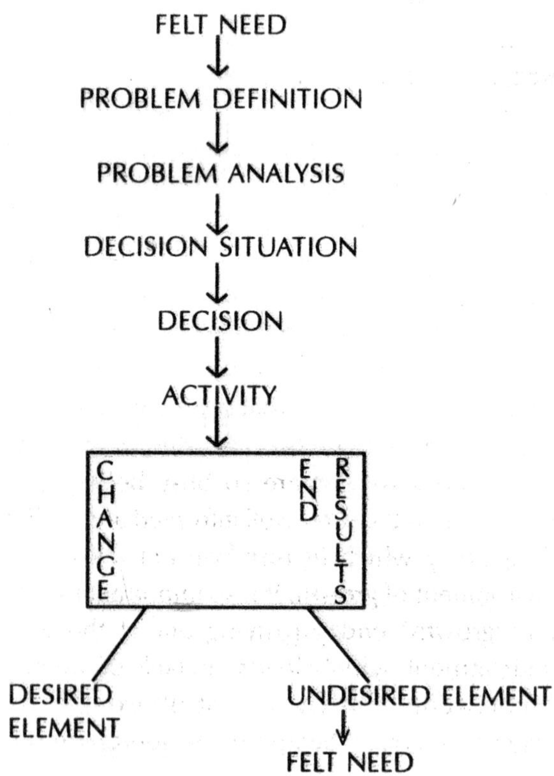

So, where does the problem lie? Very many senior officers (especially those in command of units and formations) go straight to "decision situation" without going through the first three steps. Worse, sometimes they invent decision situations so that they can make decisions. Either way, the results are that the decision will not be fully analysed - even the problem would not have been clearly understood. Therefore, a series of further decisions become essential. The other problem is towards the end of the flow: people only look at "desired elements" as the outcome of decisions. In reality, any and every decision has a few undesirable elements as a natural outcome and if not analysed properly, series of decisions will have to be taken to rectify these very results. Shortcomings in decision-making can be found virtually anywhere, especially at senior levels. Some major reasons for this are one, people wanting to "do" something during their short tenure and two, the urge to "show" results. One case (through not strictly of the Army) that explains this phenomenon (of poor decision making is the decision to make the National Cadet Corps games coincide with Independence Day. There was a vague mention that games should also be included in the NCC curriculum. This was picked up and emphasised by the then DG (in a manner totally out of proportion) and the games were conducted at a national level twice (in 1997 & 1998). If anyone has any sense in the MOD they will put a stop to this joke. Here, only the decision making is analysed:

Felt Need. There was no real need and the NCC certainly didn't feel it. During some discussions at the MOD, "games" found their place in the minutes recorded.

Problem Definition. This was a difficult area because there was no problem in the first place, given the time available and academic pressure and the fact that even PT (Physical Training) is not a part of the curriculum. The NCC simply had no business getting involved in games and, worse, conducting it at a national level. Obviously, this was glossed over.

Problem Analysis. Since the "boss" did not want to even look at the "Need" or "Problem Definition", to expect the decision to have gone through this stage is Utopian. Because even a flimsy attempt at Problem Analysis would have indicated the following:

- Academic institutions are closed till mid July.
- The process of cadet enrolments carries on till the end of August.
- Sportsmen and women are normally not NCC Cadets because of the stringent requirements.
- Conducting games to close on Independence Day was impractical if one wanted "genuine" cadets to take part.
- In Delhi this would be a very bad period considering the weather factor.
- For states short of funds it would be very difficult to find extra funds for this unscheduled expenditure.
- Because it was competition, the regional directorates would have to "create" cadets because the normal NCC cadet is not a sportsperson per se: thereby breeding dishonesty.

Note: Even an improper problem analysis would have indicated "no games" as the best choice.

Decision Situation. Another stop that was skipped because no alternatives were generated.

Decision. Having not gone through any of the earlier steps the DG "decided" that games at a national level would be held. It was really not a "decision" - it was a "whim" with possibly a hidden agenda to prove to the Army that he could do "big" things.

Activity. A decision which has not come about through a proper process will lead to unplanned knee jerk activities. So it was with this decision. Everything came to a halt, both at the directorate and at HQ (in Delhi) and all activities were related to the games. In the process, enrolment of new cadets suffered, reasonable sportspersons became NCC cadets overnight, people had to move, camps had to be set up, judges had to be found and so on. The DG continued with his whims and fancies (after all the decision itself was based a whim) and pulled out a couple of unprocessed decisions on an everyday basis. For example, to make the stadium look occupied he made all directorates put up displays at a considerable cost (which he called murals). Perhaps the dictionary was not consulted - but then whatever the senior officer says goes! He totally ignored the fact that even star-studded international athletics meets (like the Permit Meet) in India go without spectators. The end results (properly analysed) amounted to nothing substantial but some things were achieved (simply because even useless activities produce something)!

Desired Components. Since aims had not been determined (leave alone thinking about the "purpose" of the games) specific classification becomes difficult. The following could be classified as desired:

☞ The DG received some limelight as VIPs were to come.

☞ In 1997 it coincided with the golden jubilee of Independence.

☞ Some cadets (and those suddenly "put in uniform") got a chance to come to Delhi and participate in sporting events at the Jawaharlal Nehru Stadium.

Undesired Components. These, unfortunately, were large in number.

- Set in motion unhealthy competition.
- Created an environment for false documents.
- Expenditure without any cost effectiveness.
- Workload doubled without commensurate manpower resulting in neglect in a number of areas.
- Staff were perforce kept away from their workplace (schools, colleges) for long periods.
- Unnecessary expenditure on TA/DA and travel which does not show in the budget expenditure.
- Colossal waste of time.
- Unnecessary movement of transport and manpower.
- Basic aim not achieved.

The basic problem in decision making in the Army is that people do not "grow" to be senior officers. They simply get "promoted" to senior ranks.

A Personal Note. The author found the NCC games so out of context that his conscience did not permit his being a party to the games, therefore, he sought premature retirement.

Living Conditions. The living conditions are poor virtually everywhere especially for the JCOs and OR and their families. In comparative terms they are bad both on peace stations and in field areas. These conditions prevail because of lack of concern (since senior officers remain unaffected). Sometimes one wonders at the logic of say employing 50 soldiers for a full day to clear snow from a helipad so that a senior officer can land for a 15-minute stopover. In another place, in high altitude, along the border, a divisional commander got a comfortable shelter constructed to house more than 30 soldiers but the corps commander (who, needless to say, was not from a combat arm) got it demolished. His logic - in the field area there was no need to have such shelters. Of course, the corps commander did not provide a viable alternative either. On peace stations atrocious maintenance by the MES coupled with poor supervision by Station Commanders make things next to intolerable. The acute shortage of accommodation plagues the Army and thanks to poor planning (and lack of vision) there are some stations where accommodation is going to seed due to non-occupation. All in all a very unhappy state made worse by "big" talk by senior officers on "sharing poverty" and "make do with what you have" and "don't complain" and so on. The pathetic state of accommodation is a direct result of lack of genuine concern on the part of decision-makers within the Army. The Army is sick and tired of listening to spineless senior officers lamenting, "It is beyond our control" because it is not.

Travel. Travelling from the East by courier is humiliating. Because of patting each other's backs (at the top level) Air Force couriers are still playing. The Army pays for the courier and the Air Force has all the privileges. Since senior officers either fly Indian Airlines (on temporary duty) or are looked after, all is well for them. All Air Force couriers must be stopped and (like is being done now) civil airlines utilised. For going South, West, etc it is best to have an arrangement for a certain number of seats. As far as the railways are concerned quotas must be reserved in all trains in all classes. On the more frequently used routes, a combined coach (half AC 2 Tier and half IInd class 3 Tier) must be attached to all trains. The Rajdhani Express can be kept out of the ambit of extra coaches but seats/berths must be reserved.

* **Transfers.** What irks the armyman is not the fact that he is constantly being transferred but the process and the problems it entails. A problem (Transfers) that is totally internal to the Army and not well looked after because of lack of thought, lack of concern and the effort to meet undue requests. Normally everyone looks at the MS (Military Secretary) Branch who deal with officers because officers are more on view. JCOs and OR face much more of the music. A unit returns from Siachen to Leh and immediately two NCOs are sent to the Regimental Centre. For them life is very uncomfortable because it takes time to readjust. Or, a unit comes to a peace station and immediately some JCOs/NCOs are posted to HQ in field areas or to Rashtriya Rifles. There is absolutely no method in this madness. To top all this would be the lack of accommodation, no admission for children into schools and the movement itself - no one in these categories (JCOs and NCOs) have to move so frequently as in this profession. Needless to say compensation is flimsy at best. In the case of JCOs & NCOs, people responsible for creating this awful status are COs (commanding officers) and Commandants of Regimental Centres. In all this, the worst hit are JCOs/NCOs posted to non-military stations for duties with the NCC. They have (in very many places) nowhere to stay, they have to cook their own food relying on ration allowance - and have to travel 70-80 kms by buses/trains to conduct NCC classes. The JCO/NCO is a good soul - and the Army has no business taking advantage of his inherent goodness and pretending there is no problem. As far as officers are concerned, the forever groaning (due to "overwork") MS Branch acts like a Catch - 22 organisation. Often the attitude is "whatever you want, it can't be done". When you desperately want to come to Delhi they will post you to Wellington "in service interest" - and just as you have settled down in Wellington (in say 10 months) they will post you to

Delhi "in service interest". The satisfaction level is low because the environment in the MS Branch is not conducive to officer management (in terms of postings in this instance). Neither logic nor rationale applies to the MS Branch because they are extremely adept at justifying the absurd. A very senior officer today had his first experience with the field area (as a posting) as a Corps Commander. An infantry officer spent one year in field on commission. After that he could not be posted to the field till he took over as Colonel Administration of a division - but within a few months he moved on a foreign posting and is now commanding a division (needless to say, in a peace station). Yet there are very many officers who have spent almost 60 percent of their service life in field areas. But one must grant the MS Branch their capacity to justify any transfer - of course, they have the advantage of making this a one-way transaction.

Vehicles/Weapons etc. While the facilities and rules do exist, the experience of people (who can't keep following files/applications in Delhi) is that they can't get a weapon or vehicle released. Yet, virtually all ordnance officers have weapons, binoculars, swords etc. issued to them. The solution lies in ensuring at least one requirement of the soldier is met. And, it can be done.

Misuse of Authority. Far too often one experiences a complete misuse of authority. While one doesn't really talk back, it is important for people at all levels (especially officers) to realise that one always "thinks back". Pulling up people in public, being sarcastic and so on is far too common in the Army. This is detrimental to the working of any, let alone a good, organisation. Misuse of authority is extended to leave – "hold him up", "go today", "go later". Of course, there are many absurd cases - people are forced to change their wedding dates, a brigade commander does not allow a

CO to go for his Regimental conference or changes leave plans for a CO for a run of the mill sand model discussion. Even when the CO had indicated the need to go on leave three months in advance because of a family get together planned two years before! Personnel within the Army have a lot of authority which they should judiciously use. Not just for the sake of showing the existence of authority. It is in this context that the misuse of authority is seen in a very poor light by the armyman.

Ad Hocism. "Somehow do it", "Kar lo, I don't know how but do it" are common parlance in the Army and irritates the armyman no end. Exceptions are made the rule by precedent. Ad hocism continues and encourages sub-optimal functioning. Proliferation of this state is mainly due to the CYA (cover your arse) approach by all. Nobody wants to say, "Sorry, we did it last time but no more. If you want this done provide us the wherewithal".

Attitude. This sphere is a paradox. On the one hand there is the attitude of helplessness for anything and everything. For instance, very senior officers often say "we can't help it", "this is not in our hands". Who then is supposed to act? The other extreme is in the appraisal system where everyone who is initiating an ACR (Annual Confidential Report) pretends to know everything and is in full control (even when he is hiding his own weaknesses). This continuum is difficult to comprehend. Total helplessness at one end and authoritarian at the other.

Rules & Regulations. Archaic and often meaningless rules and regulations annoy the armyman. Censorship is outdated but prevalent in the Army. God knows who is trying to fool whom. Writing for the media, becoming a member of a library, applying for a passport and a thousand other issues provide an insight into absurd rules and regulations that annoy the armyman. Result: people find loopholes or simply forget to inform. One's own family, if they happen to be foreign citizens, cannot visit one without clearance and one has to fill a lot of ridiculous approval forms. There is simply no end to the stupidities we have tied ourselves to under the guise of rules and regulations.

Counting End Results

There is a great deal amiss with the way everyone treats the Army. Therefore, annoyance and anger are understandable emotions. But surely this state cannot be allowed to continue. Everything cannot be set right overnight but slowly and steadily one can hope to reach a level playing ground so that satisfaction levels improve. The armyman sacrifices a lot to do his duty well and no one should put hurdles in his path. Both from within the Army and from outside, support should be forthcoming easily and effectively.

12

Learning from the Army

A conversation about the Army with the man on the street will always give the armyman a great deal of happiness. There will always be little gems of conversation that the armyman will recall - whether it is with the man on the street or in a village or anywhere else for that matter. Reason? The outsider inevitably has something complimentary to say about the Army. Unfortunately, the general public does not make the decisions but they find a lot to emulate. Sometimes the armyman takes all these for granted. It would be wise not to do so and instead work towards strengthening those good qualities of the Army that people love to talk about. Aberrations exist everywhere but these ought to be corrected quickly while continuing to focus on the positive aspects.

The examples are there for all to see. Talk to a school principal and he or she will ask for an armyman to be the school's physical trainer and maintain discipline. The corporate person will want an armyman because he/she needs someone trustworthy. The list goes on. Though the Army has failed to capitalise on these needs of the immediate environment the least it can do is focus on what people wish to learn from the Army.

Tradition. Old-world charm and caring for "what was" permeates everywhere. People are learning to pay attention to this approach. It comes as no surprise, therefore, to see corporate houses trying to build up the concepts of tradition and permanence in attitude.

Punctuality. A PR person in a corporate house once almost jokingly asked me as to how I could stick to timings like 2.42 p.m. and 3:17 p.m.? In the same breath, he added that he could believe it only when he saw it with his own eyes. With this kind of reputation, an armyman is expected to be punctual and therefore must live up to his reputation.

Objectivity. Foreign officers undergoing courses in India are singularly impressed by the dispassionate way Army officers analyse problems of the Army and look for solutions. This permeates their functioning. In a recent interview, renowned ad man Alyque Padamsee said that what impressed him the most when he patrolled the Mumbai streets along with the Army was its utterly unemotional approach.

Helping Attitude. Openness and a general inclination to help are something this materialistic world would do well to learn from the Army. The armyman often does things just to help. Not because he weighs the possibilities of getting something in return.

In Touch With Reality. Because of the constant moves and being in different places and taking the ups and downs in one's stride the armyman is rarely living a life of pretence.

Environment. Immediate environment is always well looked after therefore wherever the Army is stationed there is always a greenery, neatness and cleanliness about the place. Look at any cantonment or any Army location and it becomes obvious. This is without the help of any extra budget too. It is basically an attitude. In places where the Territorial Army

Battalions are looking after the ecology it is a sheer pleasure to witness the changes brought about to the countryside.

Extended Family. This concept is unique to the forces and ensures a great amount of fellow feeling, trust and team spirit. Living with the Army is the only way to genuinely understand this. Relationships are difficult to fathom but they exist in a strong but informal way. Even as one experiences "contractual" relationships, all around the Army's comradeship is like an island of strength and one can only be thankful to all the people (past and present) who have made it a reality.

Continuous Updating. Tools and instruments are always ready for use. It is for this reason that one finds training and exercises always going on. Because there is such a scenario, thoughts, tactics and processes are constantly updated. True, resources are not always forthcoming, compensations have to be paid and so on but rather than make excuses the Army does its best to ensure full readiness. It is not easy with budgets dwindling every year but the Army likes having a job done well and, therefore, operational training is never allowed to suffer.

Being Comfortable. Very early in life one realises that he has to make himself comfortable whatever the circumstances and he learns to utilise all facilities available. This leads to ad hocism which the Army should take care of but Ram Bahadur or Joseph or Sundaram or Banta Singh or Hamid or Bhup Singh (the Army has them all) is an innovator par excellence.

Hardship. This is a way of life and people come to terms with it early in their careers and do not keep complaining about it. But hardships don't take away their moments of enjoyment which only an Army person can discover..............tea on the move, "churma" on a high altitude patrol etc. There are so many other simple joys that an Army person cherishes.

Being Indian. Really integrated as true Indians, the armyman is secular and without regional bias. For the common man it is difficult to comprehend this until he sees him up close. It is no small wonder then that whatever the problem and wherever it may be there is always a demand for the Army to be placed there.

Discipline. Enforced discipline is not what we are talking about but a degree of self-discipline. One academic entrusted to recommend changes in Army schools said, "The reason I have taken up this assignment is because the Army is the only organisation where discipline gets things done".

Adventure. Such activities are a part of life and people enjoy the exposure. This assists in making people more open and more team oriented. Already a number of corporate houses use adventure as a basis for training.

Leadership. An organisation where people face death willingly must have a very high quality of leadership (especially at unit commander level and below). Need one say more? The ratio of officer casualties, therefore, is the highest in the Indian context. Even the indifferent would have seen this during the Kargil briefings. The strength of the Army in cases such as these lies in the fact that at all levels leadership exists in full.

Commitment. A word that means so little in the political world, government circles, corporate houses (some are trying to inculcate this) - has a special place in the Army. Without commitment the Army cannot function effectively and it is well aware of this. Perhaps the Indian cricket team, which earns tons of money to play and promote Coke or Pepsi, would do well to study the Indian Army and its sense of commitment. The rest will follow suit.

Innovation. From booby traps to baking cakes in old ghee tins innovation is manifest all the way. Maximising scarce resources is one of the unique qualities that one develops in the Army.

Games. Virtually everyone plays some sport or the other; they may not excel but it is wonderful to see everyone out on the games fields. True, the old domination is not there but that perhaps has more to do with what sports "business" offers today.

Sense of History. In India, archaeological moments are defaced with regularity, they go to ruin, one can't even find records in the archives - but not so in the Army. Every unit is proud to look after whatever they have. So, it will not be surprising at all to find a neatly kept Digest of Service that may be over 200 years old or crockery/cutlery that is over a 100 years old. This sense of history seems to be lacking in most other spheres.

Reaching Out. The Army is always willing to share its expertise and resources without looking for returns. In areas not easily accessible one will find schools being supported by the Army or medical teams going to remote villages or assisting in calamities. In short, the Army is forever ready and willing to help out where required.

Organisational Ability. This requires the least elaboration - just think of the Republic Day Parade without any contribution from the Army; or the last Asian Games held in India. No wonder then that everyone wants the Army whenever there is a crisis: riots, earthquakes, floods, etc.

Quality of Life. Because of good communications, team spirit, the urge to live life fully, looking after resources etc., the armyman ensures a good quality of life. He works for it so don't grudge him his good life. He works hard, plays hard and lives life to its fullest.

Libraries. Contrary to what a lot of people may think, reading is not uncommon in the Army. One will find any number of well-maintained libraries in the Army.

13

Addressing Ye in Olive Greens

In the present fairly hostile environment, when it comes to actually getting things done, the Army needs to learn (and that very quickly) to look after itself in all respects. Sucking up to civilian control (we are talking sycophancy here, not suggesting rebellion) has to come to an end. Those senior officers who hobnob with politicians and bureaucrats must be removed and ostracised from the Army's extended family. It is about time we said "enough is enough" and realised that no one is interested in the Army (except in times of distress) and looking after itself and its personnel can in no way be termed as a sin.

There are far too many grey (in fact black) areas for which other than the people in OGs no one is to blame. The array of dark corners is very large but certainly not impossible to clear with vision, transparency and resolute implementation. Of course, for a whole lot of people who have been getting what they want through pulling of strings or being close to power centres the situation will become uncomfortable but a lot of this flotsam has to be thrown out of the system anyway. Genuine organisational interest must take over - not the current system of bosses (and branches) holding people to ransom under the pretext of "organisation". A word of caution: organisations are built and held together by individuals and so, anything that does not keep the (general) individual in mind will not fully succeed.

People make promises whenever it suits them but there are very few who actually follow these up. The CCPA (no less) agreed to lateral movement of people to provide more exposure and longer careers a number of years back but no ministry gave it any serious thought. Thus, no lateral movement took place. It was absurd to accept increase in career spans within the organisation but that is precisely what took place in 1998 (the retirement age was increased). Since senior officers benefited they refused to look at the effects on the "general" individual, and a heavy cloak of stagnation descended upon the Army. Even worse was the fact that the Army hierarchy was caught flat-footed with no plans despite there having been two consultancy projects carried through on the subject.

Given below is a list that should be dynamic and should be changed as per requirement (not on the whims and fancies of the Chief or some PSO (Principal Staff Officer at the Army HQ) or some senior officer down the chain from time to time.

Vision. Specific vision statement regarding the Army's place in the nation must be clearly laid down. Since the people responsible (the Government) are apparently incapable of doing so the India Army should do it on its own and let the nation be a part of it. One can hope that once such a statement is in place the powers that be (in ration shops, passport offices, telephone offices et al) will not have memory lapses when faced with a query/problem posed by an armyman. Such a vision statement will also increase all round accountability.

Growth. Whatever one does is not enough to sustain growth within the organisation. It may take 10-15 years to create an amenable environment and in order to make this happen one has to start work now. There will be no dearth of sceptics who will show you a thousand reasons why it won't work. This (lack of growth) is perhaps the single biggest lacuna in getting our due in the Army. People must be allowed to do things at their own level instead of being "guided" all the time. Blinkers need to be removed and people need to grow with a wide variety of interests, competence and skills. Genuine growth can be estimated from the capacity of individuals to fit into all kinds of appointments within and outside the organisation. The breed of senior officers who only show their importance by losing their temper or introducing restrictions need to be canned and shipped out of the Army because they are responsible for this lack of growth. This lack of growth shows up in an even more cruel manner when one finds the gallant soldiers of Kargil, at their respective levels, not doing as well as their counterparts from other arms and services, say the Armoured Corps who live protected lives (and careers) and do "well".

HR Plan, Processes & Development. On the surface the Army's HR systems are quite good but the people who make these systems work are human after all. From the macro - say the distribution of vacancies among various arms and services for senior ranks or intake plans - to the micro, say appraisal systems - there are too many slips and worse, a lot of arrogance is attached to it. For those people who keep moving up in rank "all is well" and they continuously pass advice all round. If there is a system of distribution of rank through the Army and a particular set of numbers has been arrived at, then new inputs with considerable impact must change these members. Logical, but if personalities decide to twist facts they can prove that despite the new inputs no changes in numbers is necessary. Absurd - even a fool should be able to see it but this was approved at the highest level. [Some years back, "Deprivation" and "Exposure to Risk" were added to calculate a "Fair" distribution of vacancies at senior ranks. But according to the two senior officers (from a particular arm) responsible for the study—these made no difference!!!!] This is why HR processes and plans need to be scrutinised beneath a microscope. Postings or promotions are also often highly suspect because of this lack of transparency. If an officer is not approved for the next rank the organisation does not have the courage to explain why not (too much secrecy creates a state of perpetual deception). And so, "A" gets promoted from Maj. to Lt. Col. - continues to do very well - but is rejected by the promotion board when it's time to move from Lt. Col. to Col.; "A" hasn't the faintest idea why. If he puts up a complaint the likely answer he will get is "the case has been examined in detail and it is found no injustice has been done". They don't even have the courage of conviction to say, "justice has been done". HR processes can never work if clouded in secrecy. In fact, not only should an explanation be forthcoming post facto but the system should be able to guide individuals in advance ".......you are unlikely to be approved for promotion. We recommend you volunteer for "so & so" course and become suitable for other employment" (within or outside the Army). If one can't reach this elementary level of transparency the whole HR system is a fraud and people are occupying chairs for nothing (MS Branch in particular and AG's Branch need to act urgently and thoughtfully. In all this the medicos - DGMS or Directorate General of Medical Services - are the worst). For far too long have people who are unaffected, i.e. senior officers, been making stand alone decisions. Perhaps a good case in point is making NDA entry after class XII simply because JNU asked for it. Since NDA is very different and cannot be compared with a normal 3 years in college there was no cause for change. With that one (not well thought through) decision the NDA entry moved from the "only" choice after class XI to "one of many choices after class XII". The more one analyses the more one is appalled by the pathetically poor decision making system that senior officers follow. Worse, when someone wants the decision reviewed there are a great many objections raised indicating a singular lack of desire to grow and develop positively.

HR is the Army's mainstay and the Army needs to look after it well, in fact very well. Don't take people for granted, as is presently the case. It is good to remember that heavier badges of ranks on the shoulders do not automatically guarantee brilliance - sad but true. Therefore, decisions need to be made after genuine deliberation and not just by confirmation of what has already been decided by the Chief or some PSOs in a conference room.

Train for External Environment. Suddenly one receives his orders for superannuation. This usually comes at a time when he is busy and so he avoids facing reality and then the last day looms up in front of him. Lo and behold, he is an ex-serviceman. In the meanwhile, selfish as the organisation and bosses are they will ensure full concentration at work till the last day. Result? The armyman retires but does not know what to do. The case is similar with people who have to interact with the external environment while in service - since they don't know what to do, they either do nothing or concentrate on the familiar (internal environment). Dealing with the external environment must be an integral part of all training in the Army. Reduction of specificity will increase job prospects; and more knowledge about the external environment will make it easier to deal with it so that the

Army's interests are looked after. Therefore, the Army must give its people as much exposure as is possible. This will have to be done despite all bureaucratic objections (and there will be plenty because they will feel threatened).

Lateral Mobility. The Army belongs to the nation and therefore, the whole country should be interested in its well being. If lateral movement encourages better growth and well being in the Army it needs to be supported. This would make HR systems dynamic and satisfaction levels will begin to soar. It may not be out of place to mention that perhaps the country will stand to gain as well because it will have far more dedicated people around. It is essential for the Army to demand and get a judicious share of the posts available during service as also to head committees, public sector enterprises, autonomous bodies and the like.

Bonded Labour. The armyman gives his loyalty willingly. One cannot, therefore, take him for a ride or take him for granted. He is not bonded labour! If the Army can't provide the right avenues - it has no business stalling premature retirement/releases. Except for some specific restrictions (wherein the Army has spent money and time on people getting specific expertise and the person is posted to an appointment utilising the qualification) the Army should not be allowed excuses to hold on to manpower. The Army is a huge organisation and must behave like one - going out must be as easy (for talented people) as signing up. Laying down quotas (percentages) for other ranks, that are allowed to leave each year, is absurd. Such insecurity speaks poorly of the Army.

Media Savvy. In a democracy, the media is a dimension everyone must be familiar with. The armyman must learn to utilise it as a friendly tool. At the cost of repetition it needs to be reiterated that the Army has to be proactive and learn to respect the media in a more realistic fashion. If a newspaper has to be published so be it; a magazine; a web site; anything at all so that the Army is proactive.

Network. People and continuous contact will provide opportunities for those who are leaving the system. As an organisation, the Army must encourage such linkages at all levels and all locations. Let other organisations see the Army's strengths clearly. It is this network and self-sustaining ventures that will enable the Army to look after itself. To make such a network even more effective, the Army should encourage people to leave and take up assignments. No good offers should be passed up because MOD approval is not forthcoming anyway!

Build Lobbies. There are people in various fields who are inclined towards the Army. Lobbies need to be built around them in order to generate supportive opinion to benefit the Army. This needs to be done consciously and as a long-term plan. One, however, needs to tread a bit carefully in this sphere because the politicians and power centres may use the opportunity without giving appropriate returns.

Inform People. Keep the country informed about the Army's travails, opportunities, motivations, culture, institutions, traditions et al. After all it is their Army and they have a right to know. Well-informed public opinion makes a lot of sense for the Army.

Families. There are a lot of "idiotic" senior officers who put their own opinions first and pass ridiculous orders like "all wives of Commanding Officers must be in station (for the good of the organisation) and not be employed elsewhere". To this breed I can only say that not only are they selfish and narrow minded, in the long run they are acting foolishly.

Every individual has a life of his or her own and they are all effective decision-makers - let them decide for themselves. To please a senior officer no one should drop out of circulation and lose continuity. To be able to stay as a family is a different matter and must be seriously considered along with children's education and so on. My advice therefore, is to "Look after your families" along with your commitments to the Army. DON'T get carried away by the pep talk of senior officers (who often stoop low enough to flutter the Confidential Report in your face) because they are only interested in what they are getting out of you and your families. People will obviously try to be wherever the environment is conducive to growth. Unfortunately for the Army, one doesn't come across very many senior officers who create an environment of growth. The education of children and improvement of the current status of wives must be priority work for all ranks and for those responsible for creating a suitable environment.

Institutions. All institutions, regimental, traditional, educational etc must be continuously strengthened. They must be well run and proficiently and with some degree of permanence. The Army must either train professionals or hire consultants (for suitable periods) to provide the right inputs. Administration of schools, for example, can be left to ad hoc boards (Area Commander as Chairman, some members from different directorates) ONLY if they are all suitably inclined, adequately knowledgeable and so on. Alas, this is not the case in most stations. The problem worsens when the next higher commander (having never done this job all his life) considers all this (schools, contonment boards etc) a waste of time. Unfortunate but true these officers feel that their "ranks" can overcome their lack of knowledge. The Army's institutions are really extraordinary and they need to be strengthened and preserved.

Addressing Senior Officers. All young officers should maintain diaries to note down improvements they would like to bring about when they become senior officers (one should look down on the uncommon practice of maintaining diaries only to record irregularities of seniors). The Army has too many people complaining and too few people doing anything concrete. Given the opportunity to do something solid they still complain. From among these only, senior officers have to be selected. To ensure that contact with the real world is not lost the diaries can be referred. Some suggestions to senior officers:

* Managing the external environment is more important for you (but you can do that only if you are alert, aware and educated).

* Educate yourself in an all round fashion - and keep learning.

* Remember always, people "think back" even if they don't actually talk back.

* Be fair and appear to be so. Avoid double (multiple really) standards.

* If your capacity to empathise does not show and if you can't create an environment of growth (not your opinion - and you don't have to ask; if you are genuine, feedback will come) - then, irrespective of what higher ups think, you are quite clearly a very poor senior officer. You will be surprised if you realised how frequently junior officers refer to you as "immature".

* Stop giving talks prepared by your staff officers or subordinates - it shows. People want to listen to you and not your staff and their opinions.

* Be yourself and respect people who don't pretend. There are too many "pretenders" getting promoted simply because they have learnt to hoodwink the system.

* Judge yourself by how much good has accrued to ORs families and children and move upwards.

Become Self-Reliant. There is no dearth of talent and skills in the Army and therefore, the Army must formulate "do it yourself" plans. Instead of waiting for individuals and small groups to make sense out of a mess the Army as a whole needs to look into the aspect of looking after families, ex-servicemen and their families. There is no harm in taking a leaf out of our western neighbour's Army and their method of evolving successful plans. The Pakistan Army has ensured prosperity for virtually all its ex-servicemen through profitable businesses. The AG will immediately come up with excuses as to why it can't be done – "different environment", "government support won't be there, "ours is too large a nation" and so on. He should not be allowed to get away with lame excuses - in fact, the logic should be "if they can do it we can do it even better". Transportation systems, food stores, libraries, rooming houses, adventure sports, tourism, event management etc need to be focused on. The sky is the limit. Delink from the insipid and impotent Dte. Gen. of Resettlement and become a large consultancy cum placement organisation. No one is keen (though some states are positively inclined) to look after someone else's baby - the Army must understand they are on their own. Make the best of all the opportunities.

Approvals. The Army follows the book far too seriously while the bureaucracy makes its own rules and interpretations. The Army must stop hankering for and running after approvals. It is humiliating for the people who have to run around from desk to desk. It is also humiliating for the senior officer who may not be in the forefront but it is he who is being taught "controls". If the Army responds promptly to queries and reports courtesy demands equal alacrity on the part of the government: lower level bureaucracy or Joint Secretary upward or RRM or RM or PMO's office. The Army has been accepting this rubbish for far too long. It is high time senior officers wore the pants and told people concerned "If the final approval is not received back by 'date' (say a week prior to departure) then the trip may be treated as cancelled". Same with any projects that are put up. Also, reason, for not forwarding approval for trip or not approving a project must be sought in clear terms. "Estimates seem to be on the higher side" for example should not be accepted - the bureaucracy must give a viable alternative.

Warning Note. However, this can be done if one's homework is complete and comprehensive and does not follow the usual hurried note sent because the boss wants it to go and wants it to go "today". Because, the Army's senior officers (a lot of them anyway) are not really trained to hold these ranks they try to make up by a "show of authority" - a major failing when dealing with others.

Detailed Work. With so much of wherewithal and so many really competent officers the Army frequently (much too frequently) does ad hoc studies mainly to support the boss's thinking. You (all of you who do these reports) are not helping the Army or the nation. As an example let us take a news item "India Plans Trimmer Army for More Punch" that appeared in the Statesman 5th May 99. One is not privy to the full report but analysing what has been published should prove adequate.

"Plans to cut troops strength by 20 to 25 thousand and have fewer tanks and artillery pieces:"

Questions.

Q 1. What are the changes in the environment that allow reduction of troops when commitments have increased?

Q 2. Why do units from peace stations have to move for counter insurgency duties within a couple of months of arrival to the peace station? Obviously, the Army is short of troops.

Q 3. Territorial Army (TA) cannot be employed as regular Army so what is being achieved?

Q 4. Nuclear environment or not, will counter insurgency duties, line of control, border deployment, Siachen etc vanish?

Q 5. What is the concept of "suppression" of Vijayanta tanks? If they don't work effectively they are scrap.

Q 6. "Careful pruning" of 50,000 last year, how was it achieved and at what cost? Did all senior officers reduce their large retinues?

"Shape the Army for possible nuclear environment".

Questions.

Q 1. Nuclear environment demands rapid concentration and rapid dispersal. Are the Indian Railways up to this task?

Q 2. Other than for demonstrations, where is the equipment?

Q 3. Along the northern borders where living bunkers are in an awful state for the last 30 years or more, how will they overnight become amenable to nuclear operations?

India plans trimmer Army for more punch (The Statesman : 5th May '99)

India with one of the world's largest volunteer armies plans to further cut its troop strength by about 20,000 to 25,000 and have fewer tanks and artillery pieces.

The plan to trim the 1.1 million standing Army envisages a strengthening of the Territorial Army which now consists of 50,000 part time soldiers; giving "officer-like" status to 7,700 junior commissioned officers; and the "suppression" of ageing military equipment, including the Vijayanta tank and the older medium artillery pieces.

The careful pruning - which follows a reduction in the number of servicemen by about 50,000 last year - has a dual purpose to save personnel costs and use the money to buy new equipment, and to shape the Army for possible warfare in a nuclear environment.

* The Army's armoured corps has 58 regiments, each with about 45 tanks of varying vintage: from the modern T-72s to the old Russian-built T-55s and the obsolete Vijayantas. The Army now plans to have 40 tanks for each regiment and use the 250 modern tanks thus saved to equip regiments still using Vijayantas, which can then be retired.

* Some artillery regiments, especially the ones equipped with 130 mm guns, will have 15 instead of 18 guns. The extra guns will replace older guns with some other regiments.

* About 7,700 junior commissioned officers will be paid special salaries to do jobs usually reserved for young officers, partly making up for the shortage of about 13,000 officers, mostly at junior levels.

Contd.

Contd.

* To ensure better efficiency, most junior officers will be posted out from the Army Headquarters here to the field formations. A recent paper by a lieutenant general, placed before the Army commanders' conference, argued that several hundred junior officers - usually captains and majors - stationed in the many branches and directorates in Army Headquarters will be better utilised in the field formations than as minor cogs in a vast bureaucracy. "Underposting" in some infantry battalions is one way of attempting the planned troops reduction without affecting the force. The jobs will continue to exist and the defence ministry will sanction money for them, but no recruitment will take place. Instead, the money could be used to upgrade equipment. The Army is exploring the possibility of transferring several units of the Air Defence Artillery - possibly about 12,000 troops - to the TA where they once belonged. The move will take time, as it needs government sanction and a change in TA rules. Military officials said this is an effort to slowly turn the Army from a labour-oriented to a technology-intensive force.

40 Tanks in each Armoured Regiment (instead of the current 45)

Questions

Q 1. If a regiment can fight effectively with 40 tanks why did they have 45 tanks in the first place? We can't afford such luxurious reserves at unit level.

Q 2. Even T-72s have been in service for quite a few years so what sudden upgradation has taken place to allow reduction in tanks strength?

Q 3. Total armour tactics are based on 45 tanks to a regiment. Will coverage, deployment patterns, tactics, operational plans etc undergo major changes?

Artillery Regiments to have 15 guns instead of 18.

Questions

Q 1. All instructors went hoarse explaining why regiments needed 18 guns. Do we take it that the whole Army was wrong all these years?

Q 2. How will the punishment (or TNT content) at the target end be made up? After all 17 percent firepower has been lost.

7,700 JCOs to do jobs meant for young officers.

Questions

Q 1. If the JCOs could really do these jobs officers should not have been authorised, no?

Q 2. On ground the JCOs will get more pay but the other officers will have to share the burden because everyone (especially senior officers) wants an officer to do the job. Isn't that true?

Q 3. Haven't all studies proved comprehensively that when the chips are down in operations everyone relies on young officers?

Q 4. How is the shortage of officers made up? If the JCOs in question are so good why not promote them as officers? (Fact: the JCOs will decline because being an officer implies being responsible).

Junior Officers to be posted out from Army HQ to field formations.

Questions.

Q 1. Isn't it good to learn the ropes as somewhat junior officers?

Q 2. Isn't it presumptuous to assume better efficiency with less junior officers?

Q 3. It is an established fact that older officers have set ideas. Without the junior officers who will provide fresh ideas?

Q 4. Passing the buck is common so the senior officers will miss not having junior officers to blame. Won't this lead to officers being attached temporarily at Army HQ (away from his unit and family) ostensibly for specific tasks?

"Underposting" in some infantry battalions for planned troops reduction without affecting the force:

Questions.

Q 1. Without affecting the force how can there be a reduction?

Q 2. Infantry bears the maximum brunt of all duties (operational and otherwise) so how can a study group consider "underposting"?

Q 3. It is well known that when allocating tasks units are taken into account. How will underposted units handle tasks?

Q 4. How come reduction is contemplated in the "teeth" when the Army's "tail" is too long anyway?

Transfer of Air Defence Artillery Units.

Questions

Q 1. If the TA could handle AD (air defence) then why have regular units at all?

Q 2. TA is not permanently embodied therefore won't there be degradation in effectiveness?

Q 3. Except for air defence of mechanised forces why can't total air defence be shared between TA and the Indian Air Force?

Money to be used to "upgrade" equipment.

Questions

Q 1. Isn't this whole concept a mockery? If the Army needs better equipment the nation needs to find the money.

Q 2. Upgradation is considered a joke because for years one has been hearing about the new 5.56 rifle, Arjun MBT (Main Battle Tank), computerisation etc. Aren't delays very expensive? Effectively what has been done to stick to plans and schedules?

Q 3. Isn't far too much of money being wasted by R&D, changes in requirements, producing substandard stuff which get rejected? Is there a total lack of accountability?

Labour-Oriented to a technology intensive force.

Questions

Q 1. The whole statement is silly unless it is the journalist's doing. Are we talking "labour" or "manpower"?

Q 2. Is India contemplating indifferent and inefficient bombing like the NATO or the US? That is technology - intensive - but only useful against a country that can't fight back?

Q 3. How is technology going to help in counter insurgency operations? The Indian Army does not work like the US Army who destroys and burns everything and has the audacity to justify its stupidity. Contact battle will be essential in the Indian context so "technology – intensiveness" can be thrown out.

Note: An effort has been made above to emphasise the need to do detailed (in depth) work. Too often the Army is in a hurry to see a case through. This portion may also be related to the decision-making coverage. Detailed work with a long-term effect will always be good for the Army as opposed to the plethora of decisions that are made simply because they "look good now".

Promotion Prospects. Relationship among arm/service, rank, service in rank etc need to be coordinated to ensure an effective promotion and advancement policy. Percentages to be approved for the next rank must be such as to be both realistic as well as acceptable. The system is so opaque that suspicion (that all is not well) is automatic and unhappiness prevails. Realistic parameters that must affect the profile (all ranks) are:

* Infantry must be way ahead in promotions followed by the other combat arm, the mechanised forces.

* Services will have to bring up the rear with adequate time stagger.

* Deprivation and exposure to risk must be given weightage so that an edge is clear and the aspects (of deprivation and risk) are adequately rewarded. For officers, this should be an individual weightage - for JCOs and OR this can be arm or service based. Counter insurgency operations like Siachen and Kargil mainly fall upon Infantry shoulders and they must be adequately compensated in their career advancement.

* The whole career should be chronologically (suitably) divided so that command of units comes early and JCOs & NCOs are fit for the jobs required of them. At the same time, at ranks above Brig. (included) it must be ensured that officers spend adequate time in each rank to benefit from the exposure and experience.

* Up or Out. This policy needs to be implemented but only if the Army is capable of providing an alternative career. If the side stepping is smooth the Army will have happy people in the organisation and happy ex-servicemen outside.

* Keep People Informed. All ranks have a right to know how they are doing in their careers - so keep people informed. Rejections will be easier to handle. In fact, if the branches concerned do their job well it is possible to provide each person with a very good idea of the path he is travelling.

Last Word

To the armyman the message is be fair, trust yourself and look after yourselves. Do not wait for divine interventions. Some casualties will occur but overall the Army will be stronger and healthier. If the Army has sycophancy in its ranks imagine what will prevail in the nation (think of your children).

14

Human Resource Planning and Development in the Army

Any organisation that has 980,000 people has to be extremely concerned about its people resource or human resource. And when that organisation takes on people for a full career, concern must give way to essential activity. A career in the Army leaves little time for anything other than the profession itself because of the diversity of operational skills one has to acquire. This is even more pronounced in certain crucial branches of the Army - like the Infantry.

So, how in fact does the Army manage its people? Despite the lamentations of a lot of senior officers regarding the decline in the quality of people signing up for the Army the truth is far from it. This is essentially because the extraordinary talent of the Army is its special gift to be able to convert virtually anyone into both a good soldier and a good human being. Facing death is a great learning (and sometimes chastening) experience. But do these things come automatically? Or are they achieved due to the machinations this unique organisation employs to ensure quality control of manpower? True, people are changing all the time as society undergoes changes but within the Army there is a unique brand of constancy that is perhaps based on inter-personal relationships. Yes, there are people who talk of "hi-tech" and "new millenium" and so on because it is fashionable. The bottom line is that the Army needs, especially in its fighting arms......definitely in the Infantry, people who have courage, compassion and a strong sense of commitment.

Bonds within the units create better human beings who are always willing to do a little more for others. This is basically what sets the armyman apart. Comradeship and the "izzat" of the unit is all important.....people are willing to risk death for them. Training, doing things together and for each other and other such situations create this bonding. At the micro level, activities seem quite clear cut and things quite obviously seem to be working out well otherwise we would not have had successes such as in Kargil or in counter insurgency operations. But what should be causing worry is the macro level where policies and major decisions are made. Quite a lot needs to be done at the macro level because organisationally, the Army is responsible for its manpower.

Areas Needing Attention

When a person joins the Army, he (in times to come also the women) sacrifices a lot (even if it is willingly) but in return he is often taken for granted - this is especially at the macro level. For the top brass they are simply "numbers" whose shortages or surpluses are their only concern. Firstly, the policy makers in the Army need to get educated with the basics of manpower planning (sadly, education is lacking which results in a few awful decisions). The steps for manpower or HR planning for are:

* Determine recruitment levels
* Anticipate redundancies
* Determine optimum training levels
* Provide basis for management development programmes
* Cost manpower element for new projects
* Assess future accommodation requirements
* Plan optimal utilisation

In the Army's context there is only "long range planning" (they don't have the luxury of short or intermediate range planning), therefore, all policies have to stand the test of time.

Case of Poor Planning: A few years ago, the JNU (Jawaharlal Nehru University) told the services that since the academic planning now follows the 10 + 2 + 3 system, the entry to the National Defence Academy (NDA) must be only after Class 12. Without a thorough analysis (so it would seem) the services agreed. The simple result was that entry into NDA became one of many choices after 12th from the "only" choice after 11th (earlier, the entry was after 10th and you can't find too much fault with the product, can you ? .... After all, to pose a poignant enough question, what do you think of the current service Chiefs? They happen to be from one such batch). Next, the age of commission was increased by a year. The number of years you served before retirement reduced by a year. Commanding officers (make no mistake, they play a vital role during operations) became older. No one bothered to inform JNU that the three years spent at the

NDA were academically and in terms of schedule equivalent to at least 5 years (if not more) in the learning process. And, there is no question of "minimum attendance" at the NDA. The then Director General of Military Training (on behalf of all three services) and Deputy Chief of Army Staff (T&C) were responsible for this step. Even if the Navy wanted higher education levels, the same could have been effectively taken up at the NDA itself.

Another Case of Bungling: Without proper analysis, one Chief agreed to a substantial increase in Electrical and Mechanical Engineers (EME) personnel. With the result one, we are the only Army in the world with EME (a maintenance service) larger than the Armoured Corps (a combat arm) and two, once the sheer numbers in this arm were trained the Training Centre had no recruits to train for quite a while!

Yet Another Case: Due to the lack of planning and poor (or absent) forecasting the ASC (Army Service Corps) got more than their share of ACC (Army Cadet College - or from the rank and file) officers for quite some time. RESULT: ASC had officers in a higher age group who retired early. People had to be promoted and once again, the Indian Army has an inexcusable reputation of officers of the services (ASC) getting promoted well before their peers from the combat arms (Infantry, Armoured Corps, Mechanised Infantry). An absurd situation perhaps but a reality thanks to pathetic manpower planning. And so the situation continues.

Unfortunately, shortsighted and parochial (arm or service biased) decisions leave the Army with problems that last a long time. While the top bosses are naturally responsible the staff officers who process these cases are equally to blame because they are so keen to toe the line that they tend to run ahead of the pack and create even a bigger fiasco.

If the objective of manpower planning is to procure the right people in the right numbers at the right place with the right training and in the right frame of mind this is no mean task. Since the Army takes on people for a lifetime they have to take the trouble to see that they have the right mix all the time.

So, What Is To Be Done?

* Even if specialists are available, all the policy makers need to be educated properly in manpower planning and forecasting
* Cohort-based planning should be carried out in detail
* Training has to be planned with the future in view
* Skills and requirements also have to be planned in detail
* Experience and exposure must be planned in detail
* Use of simulation-based programmes to give an idea as to how a decision will look after a few years
* When in doubt .... Ask , Ask and Ask again
* Make no decisions in a hurry
* Say "absolutely no" to opinion-based decisions
* Ensure policies are followed and that they cater to everyone in a fair manner.

Maximum dissatisfaction arises when one feels that a fair deal has not come one's way:

> **Case:** A few years back the then Adjutant General decided that a new type of commission should be introduced as an incentive to people from the rank and

file so that suitable personnel who were past the age of joining the ACC could still become officers. So, the Regimental Commissioned Officer (RCO) was introduced. On the face of it, this was a very laudable idea but because of the lack of thinking, analysis and planning, the Army was stuck with the following problems:

* If one joined somewhat late in years, as a commissioned officer he was to draw less pension than a Subedar Major with an honorary rank.

* From being a senior JCO with chances of becoming a Sub. Maj. he suddenly finds himself as a young officer in the same unit....and in the process loses the unique respect given to JCOs because of service and rank.

* All the officer-based expenses (officers' mess, extra uniforms, travel, outings etc) increase with no real returns. Not to forget the fact that he is not a young person and would have a wife and children etc.

* Of course, the expected numbers never did turn up.

An Outstanding Officer An Infantry officer (normally Infantry officers spend approximately 50 % of their lives in the field area and the other half in peace stations) on commission joined his battalion in a field area. After about ten months he was posted to a new raising in a peace station. After that he continued to move (coincidentally) from peace station to peace station until he was posted (despite protests) to a divisional headquarters in some sort of a field area. But within ten months he "had" to move on posting to a foreign country on assignment !!! On return, he commanded a Brigade in a peace station, did the course at the National Defence College, was on a staff assignment in a peace station, became a Maj. Gen. in a peace station on staff and went on to command a division in a peace station.

What really comes through is that HR is hardly getting the careful looking after it deserves. But long term usage and because at micro level people are active one gets the impression that HR planning, processes and development in the Army is in good shape. The state of affairs is far from satisfactory. Yet, because elsewhere things are much worse, the Army stands out as an example of effective HR Planning. Looking at the flaws is important because the Army is taken as an epitome of good HR management.

Most of the intense problem areas are somewhat beyond the reach of the Army but it is time people thumped tables emphatically and the Army received the support it deserves.

Within the Army

Appraisals and training must get directly linked and to this must be added well-planned development of the individual. In addition, everyone must be given the opportunity to develop skills that can be utilised outside the Army as well. Since most jawans retire at an early age, at 32 or 34, they need to be trained to step into a second career. For the officers who tend to serve for much longer, the training for adjustments in the civilian environment is virtually non-existent. *Specificity* in the Army is very high leading to a great lack of *Flexibility* for stepping into other jobs but the Army is *Committed* to look after its HR, therefore, (having slumbered for so long) the Army needs to provide the wherewithal to its people. The nonchalant attitude of "use and throw" must be shunted out and commitment towards its people must show.

Suitable housing, good schooling, steady career progress, career/professional options for families, a full (say 35-40 years) career and so on have to be ensured by any reasonable HR plan. All in all, an absolutely fair deal is expected because once a boy (or girl) joins the Army he (she) virtually hands over the reins of his (her) life to the organisation.

Reality, unfortunately, is far from the acceptable level. To say that the Army is much better than any other organisation is forcing the issue ...... we should be by far the best ...... we owe it to the gallant men; and the senior officers who make decisions, really need to pull up their socks; at present they are far too complacent.

If necessary, the Indian Army can build up its own industrial and business bases so that career continuation is also in their hands rather than waiting for bureaucrats and politicians to play ball because they will not. This is apparent even in grave misfortunes like the Orissa cyclone when they are more inclined to look at their gains. Time and again they have proven that they simply cannot be trusted. It is therefore all the more important for the Army to draw the appropriate conclusions.

Outside the Army

Since the Army is obligated to and in fact should keep a young profile the nation is honour bound to ensure full careers. Strong decisions need to be taken to ensure adequate vacancies in public sector undertakings and government jobs for those who wish to take them up.

Periodic and sporadic euphoria (and making political capital out of situations like the one at Kargil) is not enough and government and corporate houses need to embark upon a concerted drive.

One can only hope that the Indian Army will continue to be the sole trustworthy and dependable pillar of Indian society .... one shudders at the nightmare were the Army to lose its patience.

Rank and File

A brief glimpse into the lives of the thousands who line up to get recruited is called for. In a manner of speaking, the country is taking advantage of its population problem and sitting complacently because adequate numbers still join the recruitment queue. But they are volunteers and need even better looking after than if they were conscripts for short periods. Mind you, short period conscription may not be a bad idea after all. At least more people will have an idea about Army life and may even imbibe some form of self-discipline.

The recruit gets trained at the training centre, becomes a soldier and goes to a unit. The infantry soldier who does most of the tough work gets paid the least because our HR policies are absurd. Training is continuous, including technical skills, but promotions are not automatic. For each promotion they have to be qualified, successfully pass promotion cadres/tests and there have to be vacancies for them to fill. Therefore, almost 50 % of them retire as sepoys or riflemen ..... of course, a consolation prize is nowadays given as 'Time Scale Naiks' who are for all practical purposes sepoys. In each unit there is one Sub. Maj. who normally serves for 3 to 4 years; a rough calculation will tell you that in a cycle of four years only one can aspire to become a Sub. Maj. (the highest a sepoy can rise) in the unit. Of course, there are some other vacancies but giving your life for such sluggish progress is unthinkable but that is HR Planning in the Army for you.

Officers

Every now and then one hears the lament that "the Army is short of 13,000 officers" and some unthinking General tells you that it would take 20 years to make up the shortage. Only unintelligent HR planners can think of increasing the numbers of regular/permanent officers. To produce mobility and dynamism in any HR system it is essential to introduce appropriate wastage at all levels. The problem with the officer intake has always been shortage in the intake of what can be termed as support cadres. Unplanned intake (emergency commission) during 1962-'65 affected the system till the bulge was out of the system and, of course, not without dissatisfied people who had to leave once they were not granted permanent commission. Short Service Commission (SCC) officers, ACC entry (from the ranks), Special List (SL) commission and Regimental Commission (the last two are now grouped as Special Commission) which should have provided for a large number of officers always fell short. Just to give the reader an idea of the magnitude of the problem: ACC entry has 150 vacancies every year but not more than 40 actually come in; the problem is similar with RCOs etc. The solution does not lie in just filling the numbers; you need suitable people in different age groups so that induced wastage creates dynamism in the system.

Promotion examinations, competitive examinations and selection processes finally promote officers. Since the vacancies available are too few in number, a lot of fine officers are not promoted and have to bear the stigma of having been "rejected". Proper utilisation of officers is also very poor in the Army. This results in large scale dissatisfaction. Rules being what they are, channels of dissent and protest are not adequately looked into primarily because of the "holier than thou" attitude of senior officers. This sad state leads a lot of officers to go to civil courts – quite an undesirable state of affairs. Systems in the Army need to be streamlined and made credible to avoid the "run" to the courts. By and large the selection processes in the Army are quite fair and there are far larger numbers (vis-a-vis court oriented) who accept selection results with equanimity.

The problem is giving the officers a really full career. This can only be achieved outside the Army. There is no point in having a large number of superseded officers (though one has to accept that most of them continue working with equal enthusiasm and one wonders where they get it from) in the system because no promotions or incentives can be offered.

The Military Secretary's branch which plans (supposedly) the career and movement of officers always comes under fire because far too many people are dissatisfied with their functioning. The basic reason for this state is a total lack of transparency and the attitude of they know best (which they don't) and, of course, of perpetually forwarding "excuses" why they can't do any better. If this branch just throws all letters for "unusual" requests into the waste paper baskets (irrespective of how senior the writer may be) it would make their job easier. If an officer wants to be posted to Delhi (because his children are in the 10th or 12th standard) the MS branch will post him to Staff College, Wellington ..... "in service interest" and in less than a year when the officer has just about settled down they will post him to Army Headquarters, Delhi ..... yes, you guessed it right ..... "in service interest".

Needless to say that HR planning and development has a long way to go and the Adjutant General and Military Secretary need to act together and evolve workable and useful plans while keeping the individual in mind.

Roundup

If the Army created a fiasco for itself by getting stuck with Rashtriya Rifles then it is time they withdrew from the same. The objective was to give young retired personnel a career and yet have people who were properly trained. The expenditure was to have been borne by the Ministry of Home Affairs. It is time for the Army to wind up Rashtriya Rifles if it is not at their terms. This will beef up strengths in Infantry units and not upset field/peace tenures of individuals especially the rank and file.

HR is the single greatest resource of the Army and if they continue to do a "not so good job" with it the dangers lie within. If the state of society is anything to go by then deterioration, once they leave the Army, can be quite unpredictable. Both the Army and the nation need to sit up and take notice.

15

Kargil : A Few Thoughts

A lot of speculation will carry on with regard to the intrusions in the Kargil region because one of the first casualties in historical recording is truth. This becomes even more so when not enough knowledgeable people write and worse a number of media personalities give unto themselves the **authority to report accurately (sic !) without actually going into operations**. Some who really tried to go with the troops, I am sure, will refrain from writing casually just to file a story, because of the overwhelming experience they would have been through. There will also be a few who having seen the ground for the first time will express shock that such dominating features overlooking the Srinagar – Leh Road could be left vacant at any time. Well, the problem is that most people talk without having operated in those heights. Even in the best of times leave alone in the peak of winter, it has shocking weather conditions. Yet they talk without taking into account the whole picture of the defence of the country. Bungling, at any level, should of course be looked into but with understanding — because a chairbound bureaucrat's culpabality must rate very high compared to troops on the ground.

However, one aspect that has come through with great transparency is the performance at the Infantry Battalion level. Integration, comradeship, culture, tradition, raw courage, motivation, leadership et al have been of the highest order. For every hero recognised there are at least a dozen or more who go unsung, therein lies the inner strength of the Infantry. Let there be no doubt in anyone's mind .... the Kargil operations were won by the Infantry alone, inch by inch, with a great amount of support from the Artillery. The Air Force was also invaluable as a deterrent but, irrespective of claims, it has to be accepted that accuracy at those altitudes and terrain is not easy to achieve and therefore its impact on the ground is not considerable.

Understanding the Environment

It is not easy for the man on the street or the road-bound media person or the "cared for" VIP to really comprehend the impact of natural conditions on people (soldiers) in this terrain and at the altitudes being talked about. Survival itself is not easy and conducting operations is that much more difficult. When the "news" tells us about Point 4875 or Point 5210 we take it as another hill feature but the importance immediately goes up when you consider that the three main peaks of the Alps are lower (Mont Blanc – 4814, Mont Rosa - 4641, Matterhorn – 4509) than these heights. This basically means our soldiers are operating at heights where normally special mountaineering expeditions are launched and that too without the special equipment, diet or training that become quite vital necessities. All these heights are in metres, therefore, 5210 would mean 17,100 feet; and for the soldier it is not a statistical figure because he has to climb slowly, all the way, with a load weighing approximately 20 kgs and under threat of hostile fire all the time.

Being in the cold rain shadow area these features are bare rocks and not always very firm due to excessive wind erosion. There is virtually no cover and therefore, in good visibility one can see for miles and dominate the area. Except for the odd (and rare) spring there is no water available. These heights are not heavily inhabited, consequently there are hardly any roads adding to the logistic problems. The environment could hardly get any harsher.

In brief, points to keep in mind (to get some idea of the environment) would be

* **Effects of high altitude:** Lack of oxygen brings on fatigue easily, carrying any load (even a heavy jacket) is difficult, there are high chances of being affected by the dreaded HAPO (high altitude pulmonary oedema), apprehensions of sexual potency getting affected, lack of appetite, sunburns, cooking takes very long etc.

* **Effects of extreme cold and snow:** Snow blindness, reluctance to go to the toilet regularly, the lack of water (piles of snow have to be melted to produce a glass of water), frostbite, touching metal with bare hands burns the skin and so on.

* **Terrain:** The terrain is harsh, rocky, monotonous and steep. Alertness is essential all the time and, of course, the danger of injury is constantly present.

* **Acclimatisation:** Depending on the height, acclimatisation takes a long time (6 days for 11,000 feet and 4 days for each successive stage) and this is what is medically advised but to function near normally the time required is far more. If anyone is pushed against this schedule high altitude effects increase considerably.

* **Clothing & Equipment:** Anybody (I am tempted to say any idiot) can see that functioning at these heights needs special clothing and equipment. But the Indian Army has functioned uncomplainingly with any rubbish produced by the Ordnance factories because one, the bureaucrats wanted to give these factories a captive market and two, senior officers of the Army were not affected. The snow boots handed down to the Army for

so long, for example, must surely be the most uncomfortable and useless footwear to walk in (leave alone fight) and the sleeping bags are comfortable to sleep in but heavy to carry. Absolutely no R&D and no interest in making things easier for the troops! But then again, who cares??

* **Evacuation of Casualties:** This takes not only a lot of time but also four times the manpower (when compared to the plains). For the casualty the fear of not making it to the next medical post is high. Both weather and terrain often do not permit evacuation by helicopters. Sometimes lack of understanding of the situation (and criticality) leads to unique situations like an Army pilot being awarded the SC (Shaurya Chakra) for a daring casualty evacuation, and the Indian Air Force grounding (not permitted to fly) him.

* **Logistics:** All movement to carry food, water, ammunition is time consuming and manpower-intensive. Letters take ages to go and come; delays cause individual anxieties. If stocking is not completed in time there is always the danger of running short of food in winter. Needless to say, everything has to be carried up by people and where (and when) possible by mules or ponies. In our 'wisdom' air supply is rarely resorted to because it is 'expensive'. Eating the same food day in and day out can be rather irritating......don't believe the information that periodically makes the rounds that some fantastic 'ready to eat food' is being made by some laboratory and being supplied to troops because it is neither true nor is such food popular with the troops. The Army has been hearing these 'jokes' for the last thirty years or so.

* **Movement:** Imagine how slow movement would be in such an area; add to that the constant firing, shelling, casualties and the load being carried (clothing, equipment, helmets...... some of World War vintage, weapons, ammunition, food, water, entrenching tools,

sometimes construction material, sleeping bags, cooking utensils etc) and one can somewhat (it is not possible to visualise the actual even at Dras .... sipping tea in a bunker) imagine the status of the soldier. Often, he has to come down all the way to carry back rations, ammunition and so on.

Surveillance

Height differential, deep gorges and nallahs, cloud cover / heavy fog, strong winds, snow storms make surveillance of these areas extremely difficult. Other things that accentuate this problem are ..... lack of reasonable surveillance equipment, lack of capacity to 'look through' darkness/fog etc, inadequate number (when available) of night vision equipment, poor performance of batteries in extreme cold, lack of helicopters as and when needed.

Therefore, manning of the area has to be dense and multi-level (heightwise) if surveillance is to be effective. Troops will have to be deployed on the peaks, in the nallahs and midway. This, at a conservative estimate, would mean that at least ten times the number of troops currently deployed would be needed. So, all those people who periodically talk about 'sealing' the borders do so out of sheer ignorance; even in the plains this is not possible and in the hills it is totally absurd.

Satellite and other airborne surveillance (which should include thermal imaging to offset the effects of cloud cover etc) would be very useful in the area but were not available. If people wonder how we continue to be in this state despite our own satellites they would be questioning along the right lines. At the ground level adequate air effort is not made available for such surveillance and reconnaissance because priorities are not laid down judiciously. Helicopters also tend to be used far more for the movement of VIPs instead of surveillance.

Intelligence

Perhaps the real villain in the whole episode was poor intelligence. Unfortunately, responsibilities are not pinpointed specifically and an adequate number of heads do not roll. If there was an intelligence failure (which there was) people need to be sacked irrespective of where they are and which department they belong to. Historically, as a country, we have been complacent in initiating actions ...... is it any wonder then that we rate so high in corruption? Since the time of Independence, failure in this sphere has been a constant problem ...... J&K just after Independence, 1962, 1965 coups happening around us, scams, Bofors, insurgencies, OP PAWAN (Sri Lanka), political manipulations etc. The list seems never-ending.

RAW (Research & Analysis Wing) is responsible for external intelligence (anything that is outside our borders) .... and let nobody be in any doubt about that. If they are being misused by politicians in power for other jobs, then the responsibility lies with them. Other agencies like the Intelligence Bureau, local police intelligence etc have their roles clearly laid down. Operational intelligence is the sole responsibility of the Army; even when intelligence comes in from other sources, the Army has to confirm the same and they simply cannot pass the buck regarding authenticity.

With all that as a base, it must be obvious that the reluctance to share information 'in time' is the greatest lacuna. 'One-upmanship' among organisations is, putting it politely, pathetic.

SOP (Standard Operating Procedures)

The Army has a very effective way of carrying out routine jobs with the help of SOPs. They assist people to do certain jobs quickly; for example mobilisation (getting ready to move out for operations) is very easily achieved because of SOPs. Everyone knows what he is to do and when. But the snag is that the Army sometimes gets far too dependent on them, often because of some senior officers' almost emotional attachment to such lists. It is possible that in Kargil people went by fixed dates of occupying the heights and vacating them. This may seem like a foolish conjecture but reality may not be too far removed.

SOPs are good (perhaps checklists are better) but one shouldn't become a slave to them because originality is curbed and even thinking takes a backstage. Such a state will not allow people to take cognisance of changes....... simply because they don't match the SOPs. This is something the Army strictly needs to guard against.

Supporting Fire

Infantry battles, as in Kargil, are supported by the Artillery and Air Force with their fire power. Their impact on the ground, however, is greatly over assessed. This is manifest in the number of senior Air Force officers who were awarded the PYSM (Param Yudh Seva Medal) as if the Air Force efforts made any massive impact on the operations. It would be impractical and foolish to accept this as a reality; in fact, the awards have probably more to do with effective lobbying with the civilian government who MOST UNFORTUNATELY decide who has been more gallant than the other. Statistics are not important but it may be worth the while to check how many Army officers were similarly awarded (consider also that the Army's strength is so much larger and they were so much more intimately involved). This is, of course, a deviation from the main point — the impact of supporting fire.

Supporting fire is absolutely essential to demoralise the enemy as also upgrade the morale of our own troops. When our own artillery shells go overhead and land on enemy positions the sound is pure music to the ears of ground troops. Similarly, when an aircraft goes screaming over the positions held by our own troops and attacks enemy bunkers or troops it is enough to gladdens our hearts. However, it would be realistic not to expect miracles because it is very difficult to ensure accuracy. The artillery engages targets by indirect fire with the help of observers who control the fire; to expect pinpoint accuracy would not be fair. The Air Force pilot's problems are manifold: he is affected by weather, he is flying at a high speed and heights and therefore, identifying targets becomes extremely difficult. This is even when he is guided by a FAC (Forward Air Controller, who is an air force pilot operating with the ground troops). Besides, even laser-guided weapons need accurate laser illumination of the target and of course, he faces hostile fire. Rockets and cannons are more accurate but for that aircraft have to come close to the ground and the attacking time is restricted. In such terrain, as in Kargil, if a bomb or shell misses a peak it may land kilometres away (because once the crest is cleared it can land anywhere in the next valley). The percentage of shells and bombs that reach the actual target is hardly ever more than 30 %. This is still quite acceptable to the ground troops because they don't expect more. In the mountains that we are talking about, despite the Artillery and Air Force being a tremendous support, they are not the winners of the battle.

Battles have to be won inch by inch by the foot soldier .... the Infantry.

The Air Force clears out of the area before the Artillery fire commences (about 30 – 45 minutes before the attack) lest they get hit by a shell (though there is no record of any aircraft ever getting hit by an artillery shell!). Therefore, the enemy has adequate time to shake off the impact of air attacks. Now, as the Infantry closes in, the Artillery has to lift its fire to try and ensure the safety of the troops (the artillery rolls the fire so that the fire is moved ahead of the objective keeping safety in view but some impact is still felt around the objective). But over the last 200 metres (in the mountains distance is measured in time; in the Kargil area it may mean 10 to 15 minutes or more) the Infantryman is left to his own resources.

Effective and adequate fire support from the Artillery and Air Force are absolutely essential for the ground troops but must be taken in its correct perspective.

Media Coverage

The coverage and reporting on the Kargil conflict were very much improved and brought into homes thanks to extensive TV coverage and cable network. The print media was also quite effective even if some magazines had completely lost their balance — perhaps in the excitement to sensationalise matters merely in order to increase their circulation figures. For the first time, the Army was also proactive with the publications that they distributed among media persons and the diplomatic corps. All in all the, impact was very good.

However, lest people think that the coverage was universally accepted as good one needs to put things in perspective. A lot of media personalities have given unto themselves the title of "war correspondents"........ pretenders all! They may be anything but they are most certainly not war correspondents; war correspondents are those who report in the midst of war and not from the roads and protected bunkers. That's the first point that must be emphasised .... Kargil produced NO war correspondents.

We were treated to the same gun area shots over and over again ..... in a mountainous terrain gun areas are quite far removed from the physical fighting. Sure, it was a great improvement to be in the war zone at least, instead of using Second World War shots as visuals but it wasn't where the foot soldier was fighting. There were contrived shots in plenty which professionals saw through and the media people tried to fool the general viewer with .... that was deception, not reporting. Some of the more well-known networks had reporters dropping bricks all the time .... professionals (who, as a norm, don't keep writing in) smiled and the general viewer was fooled .... To the reporters, impressions were more important than honesty. A brief survey is given here:

* Soldiers in blue berets were shown going for an attack. The only troops who went into attacks were from the Infantry and all Infantrymen wear green berets and no foot soldier goes in for an attack in a beret anyway.

* Reporters talked very knowledgeably about 'special units' like ROPs ..... well, Road Opening Parties are NOT 'special units'. Any unit can undertake this task.

* One correspondent talked of throwing hand grenades from 100 to 200 metres.......must immediately get those soldiers to report to the National Institute of Sports for the next Olympics because practically one cannot lob a grenade beyond 35-40 metres.

* Interviewing an Air Force officer during a news programme, a particularly uppity anchor wanted to convey his good wishes to the jawans and airmen but since he did not know the term 'airmen' he said, "Please convey our good wishes to the jawans and 'Air Commodores' " .... unbelievable but true.

* Because it looked nice as a visual, one reporter made some soldiers walk on a ridge and photographed them against the sky. Elementary, my dear Watson ...... for soldiers, walking against the skyline is taboo because it means coming under accurate fire as they present easy targets.

Rounding Off

We also had to put up with a singer wanting to propagate pacifism. He should have stayed home, thank you .... the soldiers surely did not lose their lives to give him exposure. But India rose as one and this unification of minds and spirits helped each soldier to remember that this country is worth dying for.

A lot of questions will remain to be asked and one hopes that the powers that be are asking them in all seriousness so that repetitions are avoided. Why didn't RAW have all the information? Why did RAW miss the huge buying of special mountain boots by Pakistan in Europe? Why didn't people believe the early patrols which reported intrusions? Why didn't the brigade commander heed his battalion commanders' suggestions to keep some troops on the peaks? Why were the initial statements made without getting the full picture? The local commander (for all practical purposes) was sacked....... why wasn't the divisional commander taken to task? Did the concerned people in RAW get sacked? What about people from the intelligence organisations? We kept on hearing of the great job done by 2 RAJ RIF, but how come both the PVCs were awarded to a battalion from the JAK? Many, many more questions needed to be answered but one can only hope.

Kargil again proved the great consistency and courage of the Indian Army. One can only end with heads bowed in reverence to the soldiers who gave India a name to be proud of and to the families of those who made the ultimate sacrifice and of those with disabilities who are trying to string together their lives.

16

A Matter of Attitude

An advertisement of a foreign airline said "The universal truth is, children walk to school but run back home". So it is with us Indians, family and home are always important to us. We are not always aware of our Indianness though one perhaps feels it a bit more when you are abroad. Who is an Indian? What is India? Are not questions that are easily answerable. India is not a piece of land (or pieces of land/ islands), it is composed of many things: thousands of years of experience, kaleidoscopic images, colours, smells, rhythms and a myriad other things. There are strong sinews that bind us which we either take for granted or we try to ignore. Often, we fail to count our blessings. True, there are problems: no country in the world has had so many refugees settle as India, population growth wears off progress quickly, caste system is still practised with a narrow outlook, implementation of plans has been poor, red tape quagmire delays anything and everything and so on. But there has also been a lot of good if we care to look around objectively.

Solutions to problems we create (or are faced with) lie within ourselves. Our culture has always been capable of accepting new influences otherwise would Christanity have ever spread? In a manner of speaking it is like weather: if we had perfect weather everyday how would one appreciate good weather? Some days are better than other days, aren't they? Discontent, therefore, cannot be permanent – it cannot be one sided either . Looking at it from a TA (Transactional Analysis) point of view we should have been looking at the starting points of "spirals".

Perhaps it is all a matter of attitude (as in,"a way of thinking or behaving"). Some statements made by the publicity chief of a banned organisation (Outlook : 23 Feb 98) are, to that extent , interesting:......'to bring back the justified democratic right of the people of Assam from which they have been deprived by the Indian state for the last 50 years.";".....believe in democracy for the exploited ";".....There is no place for invoking the fear of the gun in this situation". A sort of a " I am right " ((because I say so) attitude. I cannot help but put in a little food for thought – "Bodos were the original inhabitants and Ahoms a migrant population from Yunnar and Myanmar in the 15th century."

Perceptions

If our perceptions are clear , accurate and objective, communication would flow smoothly. When perceptions are given a permanency based on misty understanding , often communications stall. When there is no communication, attitude formation is not well rounded and, in fact, would be lacking.

When we talk of perceptions or attitudes or communication, make no mistake, it concerns everyone (without exception). The insurgent, the armyman, the Police, the academic, the politician, the bureaucrat, the man on the street, the vegetable vendor at the haat, the student studying in Delhi, those utilising reservations" et al, are concerned.

The problem (to be solved internally by us – outside solutions never work) is to indentify the perception that is both objective and acceptable. On ground, however, people are playing around with what suits them. Some questions (as a sampling) that we, therefore, need to ask ourselves are—

- How close is our perception (about someone/something etc) to reality?
- Are we concerned about reality?
- Is there an element of coercion in our perception?
- How much knowledge do I really have?
- Do I enjoy the freedom and education of the rest of India and complain about lack of it in J&K or the Eastern states (when I am home)?
- Are my perceptions – issue based , situation based or relationship based?
- Am I affected by what is fashionable?
- Am I just following orders?

Authority and Delegation

Every one is very willing to crack the whip of authority, be the "know all" and so on but when it comes to accepting responsbility there are very few takers. This is always externalised. Whenever responsibility is to be pinpointed how easy it is for us to say "Not me". In group activity (as in long hierarchies) responsibility is always diffused. However, this is one area (there are some more) where the Army has a great advantage – very little diffusion exists. On the flipside, when a young boy is shot dead for a minor mis-demeanour in an ULFA Camp or three desert that camp diffusion of responsibility is so great that no one owns up that it happened.

In the area of insurgency there are decisions being made all the time and by a lot of people : individuals, village headmen, traders, organisations, the church, army personnel, insurgents, policemen, teachers, mothers and the list goes on. Only one point needs highlighting: every decision has endpoints as desirable and undesirable elements. Here , more than any where else, the tendency to overlook the undesirable creates even more problems and, in fact, starts a few more spirals of discord. Wherever a decision is made (and authority obviously exists) people must start analysing the undesirable outcomes of decisions well and cater for them.

Decentralisation of economic and other powers is also a part of this delegation process. Where this has been adequate and properly utilised, problems would be less. Simpler said than done because there are a number of influences on economic power, not the least of them – the perception of decentralisation. The point I am making is that it is possible that people hide their incompetence and inefficiency behind a "perceived" lack of delegation of power/authority.

Environment

A survey of the environment is essential but perhaps in areas with a more laidback approach to life one needs to understand what the environment "was" many years ago because the psyche has been formed accordingly. My earliest memories of the Eastern states are of the early fifties . Even as a child I was quite upset at the "haat" when I saw a trader taking beautiful hadicrafts from a tribal in exchange for a handful of salt. If the tribal distrusts the plainsman it is understandable. The innate "goodness" of people was taken advantage of. It is also well known that the concept of"locking" one's house was unheard of till very recently (in some places even today) in a number of areas. People did not like certain types of work, therefore, labour came from outside the region – be it in the tea gardens, jute or paddy or clerical work. Of course, demographic patterns were upset but it was not an external doing. The British were also greatly instrumental in isolating certain areas. Independent India, unfortunately, decided to adopt some policies, ostensibly to allow more freedom in these regions, but ended up by adding onto the isolation.

Environment has to be managed with proper understanding lest ill effects surface. In the East, people of the hills like to drink – it is a social custom. Given this environment, enforcement of prohibition seems fraught with other dangers, not the least of them is 'turning' to drugs. After a while it would lead to stealing to support the habit. These are, of course, generalised observations but, not far from the prevailing truth. This is an area where petty theft was unknown.

Development of Society

Development of a society is greatly dependent on 'Culture" which in turn is intimately linked to "Values" a society veneers. Culture is a complex of ideas, conceptions, courtesies etc, and therefore, is evolutionary in nature. Space and freedom to act are essential for development of a society. If supported by a good set of values, that society would evolve smoothly into a mature one with a high degree of permanence yet with loads of flexibility. Culture and values together influence attitudes but a myriad things influence all three e.g. education, experience, ethics, up-bringing , social circles, legends, roads etc.

Attitudes

Having taken on board everything, society or a people express themselves through their attitudes. There are a great many players who contribute to formation of/changes in attitudes; here we will discuss a few key ones.

People in General. People have aspirations, dreams, biases, self esteem, envy, pride, ego , defence mechanisms, fear, anxiety, hope, feel sorry for themselves, and so on because human beings are complex Depending on their awareness, schooling, travel, interests etc people have an attitude. Even this is not permanent in nature. Expression of the attitude manifests itself in bits. Suffice to say that it is neither simple nor predictable. How a person will react given a set of parameters is difficult to forecast.

Parents. In a generic sense, pass on biases, values, tradition, culture, percepual blocks etc. All and more affect responses and reactions.

Teachers. At school, college or later, the young are continually influenced by teachers. Teachers contribute greatly to attitude formation. A reasonable degree of responsibility is, however, not visible. Even in this group the variation is wide. Frequently, teachers express opinions that are wholly incorrect or partial truths – the damage lies in the fact that students believe them. Most teachers speak well and appear convincing; and students accept their points of view. The attitude of teachers perhaps influence the maximum because of the number who are directly influenced by them and there is an onward passage of thoughts. At a Seminar, a teacher (with an impressive following) categorically said that "anything in black and white" is the truth because it (writing or the book) has not been protested against. One can only imagine the snowballing effect of such an attitude, because we accept the freedom to publish without verification. Add to this the problem of ego which does not allow teachers (exceptions aside) to accept that they were (or are) wrong or they really do not understand.

Young Scholars. Perhaps one of the most sensitive groups because they are at a stage of opinion forming. The young won't like this – but the fact is that a large percentage of students repeat (and almost start believing) what is "in" and what is "fashionable". They are greatly influenced by coffee house "gup—shup". "They" are the future and also the present. Very few of them study the problems of the region and insurgency yet have an attitude towards all and sundry; but introspection cannot come easily to the young . When their views are also reflected by the teachers, conviction in their views become firm. Objectivity, under the circumstances, is the first casualty. One point that must not be lost sight of is that these students (those who can) readily accept all types of reservations and scolarships to study in institutions all over the country but continue to lament neglect of their region. They will soon become armchair critics from their comfortable homes and offices located all over (but their home states). This attitude of convenience is fairly prevalent. Those not so lucky will seek " **ULFA Jobs** " ——— a lot of mothers in Assam speak about keeping the young away from this avenue.

Clubs. The club culture (quite different from the club concept of Delhi etc) exists in the Eastern states and groups will vary in attitudes depending on what the focus is. Because we are looking at groups we need to remember certain aspects that affect groups like **group think** [creates, among other things, an illusion of invulnerability], **risky shift**

[due to diffusion of responsibility groups tend to take greater risks; if the group consists of risk takers then the risk factor increases considerably], and so on. Clubs (or teams) foster attitudes of their own.

Panchayats/Village Groups. Quite different in many ways from clubs, and very influential , these support attitudes that form in rural areas. In the ultimate analysis we are what our villages are, therefore, attitudes presented by these groups will indicate the general attitude. What is important,however, is that attitudes are not permanent and suffer from "group problems".

Government Employees. A very large number of people are employed in Govt and public sector jobs. Does this group also have an attitude? Ours is a jig saw puzzle in which all parts play a part to complete the image. Some peculiarities of this group are that their jobs are secure, generally permanent, they don't have to protest too much, rules are not applied to them very strictly (if office starts at 9 a.m. very few people can actually be found at 9), benefits are many etc. For them comfortable survival seems most important and the attitude of this group reflects that. They don't need too much arm twisting, by militants, to cough up bribes (euphemistically called taxes) or protection money. They know that from the administration they will not be under pressure. This group also changes colours as required keeping survival in view. The group has an attitude of convenience, unwilling to face difficulties. This is true for all insurgency hit areas.

Traders/Business Houses. An attitude of "business" pragmatism" prevails among these groups. Money makes a lot of difference in "reflected" attitude. In Assam, for example. the "Marwaris" were never "unwanted" because they could "pay". Without money no militant organisation can function, therefore, the business groups (in addition to the foreign hand and administration) are responsible for "Continued insurgency". One could surmise that this is an"anti national attitude". True but only partially because business house and traders do not look for people to give money – they do so because they feel they can continue to make money in this way. Needless to add, the loser is the man in the street because all "extra" costs are passed onto him.

Foreign Hand. There are countries and organisations that would not like India to prosper and progress to achieve her potential. Altering the demographic balance, keeping areas under turmoil, interfering with trade balances – whatever it takes, they feel the means are justified. "Attitude of intervention would be a reasonable assumption. Since it does not cost very much (both in lives and money) it is, in their opinion, a good choice. Our free democray and innate sense of complacency assists them further. Safe havens across the borders provided to militants may sometimes prove to be adequate support. From this attitude, militant groups receive encouragement.

Human Rights Activists. Organisations and activists fighting for human rights must have reasons for what they are doing (beyond being simply fasionable). Unfortunately, focus and achievements are rarely very clear. They seem to show greater interest in regular organisations (security forces) and making passing references to militant organisations – possibly they feel safer doing so. Loud proclamation of credentials is, in my opinion, always suspect and a lot of them do fall in that category. I have been trying to find out, albeit without success, about human rights activists or organisations working in Taliban held Afghanistan or Pakistan Occupied Kashmir (POK). What comes through is an "attitude of morality " (with "safety first") – talking at international conferences, quoting statistics that are not validated etc etc.

Media. The oxygen for militants is media. Without media prop up such organisations would wither. Since media hankers for stories that make "news" truth frequently becomes a casualty. The whole truth does not make a story – the establishment does not make a story — going to a militant hideout (however, antinational it may be) is a story, anti establishment is a story, breaches of discipline in uninformed forces is a story. To be fair, all types of media may not fall under this generalisation but the print media does. Detailed knowledge seem unnecessary to most correspondents, they feel "language" will make up the rest. Sad but true, most correspondents are neither willing to learn (it would mean they don't know) nor willing to experience. (Reminds me of the Indian "War" correspondent who came to our HQ about ten days after the 1971 war was over). The attitude of "I know it all" certainly has its pitfalls not the least of them being misinforming the public .

Judiciary. The judiciary dispenses justice in a "normal" fashion in "abnormal" circmstances. How does one push fit an attitude on this manner of looking at problems . Take for example, the feelings of a company commander who hands over four militants classified "black" (who were apprehended with weapons while firing at a patrol) only to find them out on bail three months later. For people who understand the environment of insurgency, bail means nothing because everyone jumps bail. Why does this happen? Surely, it could not be fear; perhaps it is a lack of concern for ground reality. It is, in a manner of speaking, an attitude of indifference (to relate to the special circumstances).

Administration. An interesting situation because everything can be blamed on "abnormal" circumstances. Excuses galore are available for roads not being repaired, rations not being available, flood control measures failing – the list is all encompassing. Except where personal safety is threatened (if at all), for the administration it is less work than usual. An attitude of helplessness prevails.

Politicians. Because of the business they are in, and with unpredictable tenures, an attitude of make hay irrespective of the sun would suffice to describe their predicament. Enough is written in the media, as it is, about linkages,finances, kith and kin etc, therefore, repetitions are unnecessary. Of course, they are required to make appropriate noises depending on how the wind blows and how the pressures rise.

The State Police. Basic law keepers of the state are quite happy to play second fiddle because responsibilities have got dispersed. Continuous and updated intelligence should be available with them but very little is forthcoming. Yet it is not as if they are not busy. Sometime back I had to take a lift in a goods carrying truck along a highway partly through Meghalaya and partly in Assam. The driver stopped his vehicle every now and then and the cleaner went bounding into a police post and was back in the truck with equal speed. I was intrigued –"why so many check posts?" The reply I got was quite revealing: "Sahb, I am carrying only Maltova and that also well below the tonnage I am allowed to carry, but if I don't pay at all these posts they can waste a lot of my time. I end up paying , for such a trip, Rs 2,500 or more between Guwahati and Aizawl." From some police posts, without a shot being fired all the weapons are taken away. There are instances (not so common) of people walking across to militant organisation with their weapons for the money offered. Yet, this is certainly not applicable across the force. So how does one identify "an" attitude —— a complex attitude?

Central Police Forces. A large number of them are deployed for long periods in one or the other insurgency areas. Methods are police oriented even if functioning is sometimes different. They are often short on patience, therefore, (sometimes) they attract the label of being high-handed. Their senior officers are not very visible to the units, possibly due to their organisation. Since a lot of them feel that their next move may be to another insurgency hit area a sort of inertia exists. An attitude of boredom, therefore, is understandable.

The Army. Expecting all to fit into any slot is built into the Army structure and thinking. To an extent this is correct because versatility is the basic strength of an Army man. Everyone is expected to do a thorough and competent job. Again, not wrong, but circumstances change fairly quickly which demand great flexibility as also updated knowledge. Since the Army is used to judging performance by results sometimes the focus shifts to results only. This induces aberrations which could easily be avoided if performance was assessed by qualitative means. Having arrived at a place units start "learning" – about the terrain, people, customs, militant groups, modus operandi and so on. In the process their tenure is up and they are on their way. The attitude is of learning and performing all the time. The emphasis on performance is so high that people do not have the time to "understand" the people, tradition, culture and communication blocks.

Insurgent Groups. Most of them seem to have started a game they can't finish. Periodically they have to think of their grandiose dreams – however elusive they may be – and remind people. Ideological commitment is not very common to find. In fact, even within the groups a fair degree of coercion and threat have to be used to keep the cadres in line. Desertions are not uncommon. For a great number it has become a means of livelihood or a means to take revenge. The glamour bit wears off fairly quickly too (guns, guitar and girls don't last). Groups give different names to make money (goodwill, money, taxes, windfall money etc) and some distribute the money as per stature while some do it on an as required basis. So what then is the attitude of an insurgent group? It is not singular in nature. The senior leaders want to play God within the groups as well as outside –democracy as per their diktats. The middle rung is in a situation –"can't leave : can't go up". The recruits or junior lot would be happy to change to another job. An attitude of confusion could best describe the state.

Effects

Manifestation of all these attitudes present a complex picture of a chariot being drawn in different directions; everyone claiming that he/she is pulling in the correct direction. A brief list of effects (without analysis) is given below:-

* The feeling of isolation deepens.
* Tendency to externalise all that is unpalatable.
* Power seekers are many (Not many want to give up powers).
* Gun culture.

* Easy money is available (grants, extortions, drugs etc). Perhaps the collections would have gone up as a result of the Pay Commission"
* Industry does not come into the region.
* Less and less jobs
* Seeking benefits but not responsibilities
* Politicians keep crying for more autonomy (the people can't eat autonomy but militant leaders find that fashionable) when they should be demanding more developments.
* Agreements are rarely implemented.
* No cost benefit analysis is ever done. Take the demand for introduction of "inner line" for example.
* Development that should have taken place hasn't come about: say fruits (fruit based industry/trade), exotic foods (herbs, bamboo shoots) floriculture, furniture, hydel projects, spices, coffee etc .
* Academic slide takes place by sticking to old curricula and systems as also many closures.
* Organisations like the Church, YMA (Young Mizo Association) have not broadened their aims and interest despite large following.
* Non-acceptance has become a norm and tolerance levels low.
* Slash and burn cultivation (Jhuming) still continues.

* Immense losses (oil pipe destruction, railway disruptions etc) have basically affected the region.

* Communiucation are still poor.

* Drugs availability and trade have increased.

Congruency

Despite all the conflicts of interests, congruency needs to be found so that people's quality of life improves. Impossible one would say, given the contradictions listed above but it is possible. Once we take stock of the contradictions commonalities will be found. One sure base to start on is that everyone is looking for a better future of the region (yes, even a culthroat businessman's self interest demands a better future – at least in buying power). Methodologies and approaches (even paths) may differ but ultimate commonality exists. Megalomaniacs aside very few want to follow a path of destruction.

People have to say "enough is enough" and they have to become more rational in their expectations. There is a need to get rid of "they syndrome" and start looking at what "we can do". This is applicable to all in every context people must ask (and not fear the gun all the time) the militant group leaders to show at least one long term plan that they have executed successfully. Student groups and the young will have to act for the future and not look for quick fix solutions or for doles or depend on reservations. In places like Delhi when one meets and sees students from insurgency hit areas there are no signs of lack of money or lack of support - but they still complain a lot. A lot more of introspection is called for if we are to find an acceptable common path.

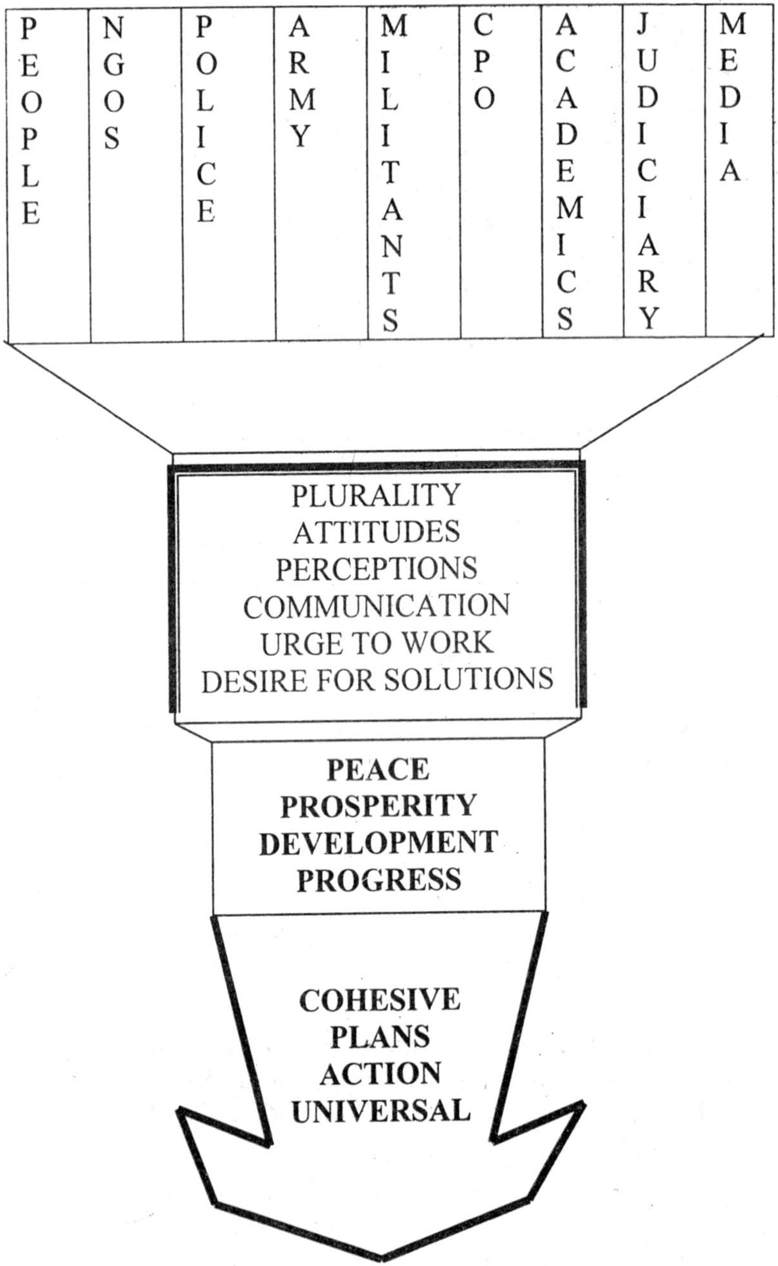
PEOPLE
NGOS
POLICE
ARMY
MILITANTS
CPO
ACADEMICS
JUDICIARY
MEDIA
PLURALITY
ATTITUDES
PERCEPTIONS
COMMUNICATION
URGE TO WORK
DESIRE FOR SOLUTIONS
PEACE
PROSPERITY
DEVELOPMENT
PROGRESS
COHESIVE
PLANS
ACTION
UNIVERSAL

The cynical and the sceptics will always be there but we need to take them less seriously. Any solution that appeals to the general public, who are looking into the future, should be followed up seriously.

Conclusion

> **"`We are' in terms of history, and history must reckon with this `we are' which must, in its turn, keep its place in history. I have need of others who have need of me and each other".**
>
> **Camus**

Academics will always find it fashionable to talk of a "birthright to rebel". Fair enough, but they should hasten to add "with a purpose". Impressive lectures and theories are often not enough to keep the hearth warm and the bellies full. Therefore, rational and purposeful development are essential.

The cacophony of varied attitudes (of coercion, of confusion, of convenience and so on) will remain because people are different but a positive attitude and an attitude of common sense must emerge. Narrow self interests (or small group interests or large group interests) can never yield results of a permanent nature. One must look at the positive side more often - despite the remoteness and perceived lack of development one has never heard of a starvation death in the North East (this is the first usage. I do not like the clubbing together of the seven very different states). There are states where codes of conduct are still followed in letter and spirit.

Like human beings, a country also keeps growing and evolving. If everything is not right today it will be, tomorrow or the day after. Sometimes we lose our way but we need not be lost as long as we know where we are going. Similarly, planning and execution will go hand in hand as long as we accept `ownership' of decisions we make. Professionals and non professionals alike have to put their shoulders to the wheel and make progress possible. The hero in all this is the common man who faces life squarely, there are no external solutions to internal problems. The shift has to be made towards conflict resolution and problem solving. We would do well to remember the age old saying "when you point a finger at someone, remember that, at least, three fingers are pointing at you."

It is really a matter of shaping and making our attitude work for us - the more positive the better. We could pray:

"Sarve bhai sukhine shantu

Sarve shantu niramayah

Sarve bhadrani pashantu

Ma kaschid duksham apnuat"

["May all be happy, may all be healthy, may all see only the good and may sorrow come to none"]

After all, it is only a matter of attitude.

Some Facts & Figures of Interest About the Army

(Indian Defence Year Book 1998-99; The Military Balance)

(Ministry of Defence Annual Report and other published material)

Strength

* Personnel : 980,000 [Total All Three Services 1,145,000]

  Navy : 55,000 Air Force : 110,000

  Army 85.6 % Navy 4.8 % Air Force 9.6 %

* Commands : 5 (Regional Commands or Field Armies)
* Corps : 11
* Armoured Divisions : 3 [2 to 3 armoured brigades and 1 SP (Self Propelled) artillery brigade]
* RAPID Divisions : 4 [2 infantry brigades and 1 mechanised brigade]
* Infantry Divisions : 18

* Mountain Divisions : 9
* Artillery Division : 1
* Independent Armoured Brigades : 5
* Independent Infantry Brigades : 7
* Independent Mountain Brigades : 2
* Parachute Brigade : 1
* Independent Artillery Brigades : 3
* SSM (Surface to Surface Missile) Regiment : 1 (Prithvi)
* AD (Air Defence) Brigades : 18
* Engineer Brigades : 3

Combatant Units

* Armoured Regiments : 59
* Infantry Battalions : 355 [Including 25 mechanised and 10 para/commando]
* Artillery Regiments :190 [1 SSM, 2 Multiple Rocket Launcher, 50 Medium, 69 Field, 39 Mountain, 29 AD]
* SAM (Surface to Air Missile) :2 groups with 15 SAM regiments
* Helicopter Squadrons : 14 [anti-tank and air observation]

Territorial Army Units

* Infantry Battalions : 25
* Departmental Units : 29

Equipment

* Main Battle Tanks (MBTs) : 3314

  T-55 - 700

  T-72 - 1400

  Vijayanta - 1200

  Arjun - 14 (numbers would have gone up)

* Reconnaisance and APCs (Armoured Personnel Carriers)

  BRDM - 100

  OT 62/64 – 157

  BMP1/2 - 1450

  Towed Artillery 4175 pieces

  1115 75mm

  1350 105mm

  550 122mm

  750 130mm

  410 155mm

* SP Artillery 180 [80 x 105mm and 100 x130mm]
* Multiple Barrel Rocket Launchers : 150
* Mortars 1200 [500 x 120mm and 700 x 160mm]

In addition, each Infantry Battalion has 6 x 81mm mortars

* Anti-tank Weapons Anti-tank missiles (Milan etc)

  84 mm rocket launchers (Infantry units)

  106 mm recoilless (Rcl) rifles (Infantry)

* AD (air defence) Guns 2400 (23mmZU and 40mm)

* SAM (Surface to Air Missiles) Approx 1800 (SA-6, SA-7, SA-8, SA-9,

  SA-13, SA-13)

* Surveillance Radars

* Helicopters 200

* Landing Craft 2

Other Forces

* Assam Rifles : [Ministry of Home] 52,500 (31 battalions)

* Rashtriya Rifles : [Ministry of Defence] 40,000 (36 battalions)

* NSG (National Security Guards) : [Cabinet Secretariat] 7,400

* ITBP (Indo-Tibetan Border Police) : [Ministry of Home] 32,200 (28 units)

* SFF (Special Frontier Force) : [Cabinet Secretariat] 9,000

* BSF (Border Security Force) : [Ministry of Home] 185,000 (150 units)

* CRPF (Central Reserve Police Force) : [Ministry of Home] 165,300 (130-135 units including 10 Rapid Action, 2 Mahila)

* DSC (Defence Security Corps) : [Ministry of Defence] 31,000

* State Armed Police (400,000) ; Central Industrial Security Force (88,600) ; Railway Protection Force (70,000) ; Home Guards (472,000) ; Civil Defence (394,000) ; Special Protection Group (3,000) and, of course, the Police

DEFENCE EXPENDITURE

(In Crores)

Department	1996-97	97-98	98-99	1999-2000
DDP & S	727.60	1067.29	728.43	613.95
R & D	1535.79	1951.38	2299.80	2773.00
Navy	3976.22	4764.56	6191.29	63.45
Air Force	7492.30	9126.83	9189.78	10278.66
Army	15873.16	18367.93	22790.70	25264.94
Total	**29505.07**	**35277.99**	**41200.00**	**45694.00**

DDP & S : Department of Defence Production & Supplies

R & D : Research and Development

Strengths & Budgets

Strength : Army 85.6 % ; Navy 4.8 % & Air Force 9.6 %

Budget : Army 55.3 % ; Navy 14.8 % & Air Force 22.5 % [Others 7.4 %]

[1999-2000]

SHARE OF GALLANTRY AND DISTINGUISHED SERVICE AWARDS

[Awards announced on 26th January 1998 as an example: Total : 309]

Army : 203 ; Navy : 42 ; Air Force : 59 ; Others : 5

Vishisht Seva Medal (VSM) Awarded : 97 (including one Bar to VSM which means being awarded the same award again)

Army - 54 Navy - 16 Air Force - 25 Others - 2

Posthumous Awards Army - 26 Navy - Nil Air Force - Nil

Note : A brief review to raise queries about the awards system and question the justification of compensations and rewards vis-a-vis reality. Compare allowances (say flying and counter-insurgency) and facilities (say periods spent in peace stations and number of days spent away from home etc).

TRAINING INSTITUTIONS

* Sainik Schools, Military Schools, Rashtriya Indian Military College

* National Defence Academy (NDA) #

* Training Centres (various Infantry regiments, arms, services)
* Officers Training Academy (OTA)
* Indian Military Academy (IMA)
* College of Combat
* The Infantry School
* Defence Services Staff College (DSSC) #
* High Altitude Warfare School (HAWS)
* Counter Insurgency and Jungle Warfare School (CIJWS)
* College of Defence Management (CDM) #
* Each arm and service also has a training establishment like the College of Military Engineering (CME), College of Materials Management (CMM) and so on.
* Tri-service institutions

Journals and Magazines

Some of the publications that interested people can read are :-

Combat Journal

Infantry Journal

USI Journal (incidentally this journal has never changedits design and format since its first publication) USI was established in 1870

Trishul (published by DSSC)

R&D Digest

Defence Management (published by CDM)

Pratividrohi (published by CIJWS)

Publications of IDSA (Institute for Defence Studies and Analysis)

Publications of other institutions (of various arms and services)

Who to Contact for Information & Material

* Army Public Relations Officer

  South Block

  Army Headquarters

  DHQ PO

  New Delhi 110 011

* Additional Director General of Recruiting

  Army Headquarters

  West Block III

  R K Puram

  New Delhi 110 066

Select Bibliography

* Traditions of the Indian Army - Dharam Pal [Publications Division of Ministry of Information and Broadcasting 1961]
* Battle Honours of the Indian Army - Maj Sarbana Singh [Vision Books 1993]
* The Indian Army - Lt. Gen. S.L. Menezes [Viking 1993]
* The Army in India and its Evolution [Anmol Publications 1985 Reprinted]
* The Indian Army - Stephen Cohen [Lancer International 1990]
* Organisation and Administration in the Indian Army - Brig Rajendra Singh [Army Educational Store 1980]
* India's Army - Maj Donovan Jackson [Sampson Low, Morston & Co Ltd, London 1940]
* Sons of John Company (Indian and Pakistan Armies 1903-1991) – John Gaylor [Lancer International 1993]

* Indian Army After Independence - Maj K.C. Praval [Lancer International 1993]

* India and its Army - Rajesh Kadian [Vision Books 1990]

* Forging the Shield - Lt. Gen. P.S. Bhagat, VC [Statesman 1965]

* Indian Army - N. Kunju [Reliance Publishing House 1991]

Indian Army Chiefs

* Field Marshal K.M. Cariappa, OBE 1949-53
* General Maharaj Rajendra Sinhji, DSO 1953-55
* General S.M. Shrinagesh 1955-57
* General K.S. Thimaya, DSO 1957-61
* General P.N. Thapar 1961-62
* General J.N. Chaudhuri 1962-66
* General P.P. Kumaramangalam, DSO 1966-69
* Field Marshal S.H.F.J Maneckshaw, MC 1969 73
* General G.G. Bewoor, PVSM 1973-75
* General T.N. Raina, MVC 1975-78
* General O.P. Malhotra, PVSM 1978-81
* General K.V. Krishna Rao, PVSM 1981-83
* General A.S. Vaidya, PVSM, MVC & Bar 1983-86
* General K. Sundarji, PVSM 1986-88
* General V.N. Sharma, PVSM, AVSM 1988-90
* General S.F. Rodrigues, PVSM, VSM 1990-93
* General B.C. Joshi, PVSM, AVSM 1993-94
* General S. Roychowdhury, PVSM 1994-97
* General V.P. Malik, PVSM, AVSM, ADC Since 1997

Afterthought

A few items that have recently appeared in the press need to be referred to so that meaningful debates emerge. They are :

Bharatpur: The fire at the Bharatpur Ammunition Dump and the ensuing loss is inexcusable. Of course, a court of inquiry will surely apportion blame but only the people now in charge will be made responsible for the flaws. The malaise, however, is deeper because all those VIPs who have gone there for inspection (and a visit to the bird sanctuary) and done nothing about safety and security need to shoulder the blame squarely. It is stupid to say that for want of finances fire lanes had not been created or inflammable material like plastics were used to protect the ammunition from rain or adequate care was not taken to ensure that electricity lines were not close to the ammunition or adequate fire fighting equipment was not available (in time). If any bureaucrat (civilian or in olive green) delayed or laid priorities which resulted in inadequate preparedness he (or they) need to be punished and the same publicised. This is not to say that people currently in charge should get away....certainly not... but disciplinary action should not be restricted to them.

- **Stealing the affection of a brother officer's wife:** This is a unique clause that applies to service officers and must continue to do so. It is heartening to know that people who cross the line have to leave the force. If a corps commander has recently been asked to put in his papers and leave, it is at least indicative that the Army is willing to take action against the erring persons. In the Army people are frequently in field and families are on their own; secondly, pure comradeship is critical for effective functioning, therefore, tampering with relationships is inexcusable. Culpability is even higher with senior officers (because they are perpetually giving moral lectures and are supposed to be role models) and perhaps they deserve more severe punishment.

- **Playing favourites:** Rumours will always make the rounds if there is even a slight bit of truth linked. Currently, one hears that the Chief wants a particular Maj Gen, who has not been cleared for the next rank by the selection board, to be promoted. This is a very poor example of effective functioning (if there is some truth in it) because one, the Chief does not trust the judgement of a collective body and gives unto himself extra constitutional powers and two, he throws himself open to be manipulated by the Ministry (read bureaucrats and politicians). One hears that this is also happening in this instance: another Maj Gen who has not been approved for promotion but has adequate political clout to look for a quid pro quo......the Chief's favourite getting the nod subject to the Chief not objecting to this Maj Gen also being promoted. If there is any truth in this story, that is making the rounds, some in house cleaning up is required and certainly a lot of soul searching for the senior officers, Chief downwards, who make decisions.

- **Sri Lanka:** Media has recently stated that India may have to get involved in trying to resolve the Sri Lankan crisis. Even before the reports appeared in the press the Army should have categorically stated that they are unwilling to be taken for a ride again to resolve a situation created by poor policies, poorer diplomacy and rank bad politics. Should some unavoidable requirements come up, the Army must ensure that all activities are as per their choice, as per their state of preparedness, as per their timings and, most importantly, they must not go by any other organisation's intelligence assessment. It is time the Army started looking at lives more seriously.

- **Kargil:** Hearing from people who have been through the operations (obviously, no names can be mentioned lest a witch hunt starts) it seems the Army needs to carry out a really objective assessment of planning, execution and what the forward troops really felt. They can do it in house but must introduce corrective measures immediately. There is a lot of unhappiness (and sadness) at the cutting edge about the way the operations were conducted. It must not be necessary to throw the rule book or flutter the appraisal form at people to get them moving. They must do so because they are convinced and they have the trust in the hierarchy........sadly, it is emerging that these were missing. The Indian Army owes it to the gallant soldiers who gave India her "izzat" back at Kargil. Also a silent prayer for those who did not come back. After Kargil it can not be "business as usual" and the Army must ensure that.

- **Officer Planning:** One is horrified to hear about cashing in on Kargil and increasing intake in the officer cadre. This may result in 6 to 7 subalterns being posted together to a unit. Imagine what will happen 15 years hence when they come up for promotion (the first selection rank); the rejection rate and, therefore, dejection would be very high. Only absolute ignoramuses can think of solving the problem of numbers like this. But then one must accept that most of our decisions are not thought through and lack vision. Is it something to do with growing senior officers who cannot visualise the future or think ? Increasing support streams, who leave the system quicker (having received a fair deal), is sensible but increasing regular intake (from the Indian Military Academy) beyond the numbers that the system can absorb is foolish. It indicates lack of elementary knowledge of manpower planning.

Index